Editor

Sara Connolly

Managing Editor

Ina Massler Levin, M.A.

Illustrator

Kevin McCarthy

Cover Artist

Brenda DiAntonis

Art Production Manager

Kevin Barnes

Imaging

James Edward Grace

Rosa C. See

Publisher

Mary D. Smith, M.S. Ed.

NONFICTION COMPREHENSION *Science*

Grade 3

Ideal for **Test Practice**

Author

Ruth Foster, M.Ed.

Teacher Created Resources, Inc.

6421 Industry Way

Westminster, CA 92683

www.teachercreated.com

ISBN-1-4206-8021-8

©2006 Teacher Created Resources, Inc.

Made in U.S.A.

Teacher Created Resources

Table of Contents

Introduction

* **Science is thrilling.**

  Think of snakes with special pits to detect prey by sensing heat.

* **It has changed our world.**

  Think of how clothes are being made that are stronger than steel.

* **It affects our lives daily.**

  Think of how sharing water with predators can reduce the occurrence of Dengue fever.

Reading comprehension can be practiced and improved while coupled with science instruction. This book presents short, fascinating science stories. The stories were chosen to incite curiosity, augment basic science facts and concepts taught at this grade level, and introduce a world of ideas, people, and animals.

A page of questions follows each story. These questions will provide a child familiarity with different types of test questions. In addition, the practice they provide will help a child develop good testing skills. Questions are written so that they lead a child to focus on what was read. They provide practice for finding the main idea as well as specific details. They provide practice in deciphering new and unknown vocabulary words. In addition, the questions encourage a child to think beyond the facts. For example, every question set has an analogy question where students are expected to think about the relationship between two things and find a pair of words with the same type of relationship. Other questions provide an opportunity for the child to extrapolate and consider possible consequences relevant to the information provided in the story.

The book is written so that writing can be incorporated into every lesson. The level of writing will depend on what the teacher desires, as well as the needs of the child.

Lessons in *Nonfiction Reading Comprehension: Science* meet and are correlated to the Mid-continent Research for Education and Learning (McRel) standards. They are listed on page 8.

A place for *Nonfiction Reading Comprehension: Science* can be found in every classroom or home. It can be a part of daily instruction in time designated for both reading and science. It can be used for both group and individual instruction. Stories can be read with someone or on one's own. *Nonfiction Reading Comprehension: Science* can help children improve in multiple areas, including reading, science, critical thinking, writing, and test taking.

Using This Book

The Stories

Each story in *Nonfiction Reading Comprehension: Science* is a separate unit. For this reason, the stories can but do not have to be read in order. A teacher can choose any story that matches classroom activity.

Stories can be assigned to be read during either science or reading periods. They can be used as classroom work or as supplemental material.

Each story is five paragraphs long. The stories contain 325 to 350 words. They are written at grade level with appropriate sentence structure.

New Words

Each story includes a list of eight new words. Each of the new words is used a minimum of two times in the story. New words may sometimes have an addition of a simple word ending such as "s," "ed," or "ing." The new words are introduced in the story in the same order that they are presented in the new word list. Many of the new words are found in more than one story. Mastery of the new words may not come immediately. Practicing articulating, seeing, and writing the words will build a foundation for future learning.

* A teacher may choose to have the children read and repeat the words together as a class.

* While it is true that the majority of the words are defined explicitly or in context in the stories, a teacher may choose to discuss and define the new words before the children start reading. This will only reinforce sight word identification and reading vocabulary.

* A teacher may engage the class in an activity where children use the new word in a sentence. Or, the teacher may use the word in two sentences. Only one sentence will use the word correctly. Children will be asked to identify which sentence is correct. For example, one new word is *rodent*. The teacher might say,

  "Rodents are small animals like mice and rats that have sharp teeth for gnawing."

  "Rodents are big animals like bears and lions that like to play with snakes."

* A teacher may also allow children to choose one new word to add to their weekly spelling list. This provides children with an opportunity to feel a part of the decision-making process as well as to gain "ownership" over new words.

In addition, practice spelling sight words reinforces the idea that we can learn to recognize new words across stories because there is consistency in spelling.

* A teacher may choose to have children go through the story after it is read and circle each new word one or two times.

Using This Book (cont.)

The Writing Link

A teacher may choose to link writing exercises to the science stories presented in the book. All writing links reinforce handwriting and spelling skills. Writing links with optional sentence tasks reinforce sentence construction and punctuation.

✳ A teacher may choose to have a child pick one new word from the list of new words and write it out. Space for the word write-out is provided in this book. This option may seem simple, but it provides a child with an opportunity to take control. The child is not overwhelmed by the task of the word write-out because the child is choosing the word. It also reinforces sight word identification. If a teacher has begun to instruct children in cursive writing, the teacher can ask the child to write out the word twice, once in print, and once in cursive.

✳ A teacher may choose to have a child write out a complete sentence using one of the new words. The sentences can by formulated together as a class, or as individual work. Depending on other classroom work, the teacher may want to remind children about capital letters and ending punctuation.

✳ A teacher may require a child to write out a sentence after the story questions have been answered. The sentence may or may not contain a new word. The sentence may have one of the following starts,

- I learned . . .
- I thought . . .
- Did you know . . .
- An interesting thing about . . .

If the teacher decides on this type of sentence formation, the teacher may want to show children how they can use words directly from the story to help form their sentences, as well as make sure that words in their sentences are not misspelled. For example, this is the second paragraph in the selection titled Snake Sense.

Rattlesnakes are a type of pit viper. Pit vipers are snakes with special openings on their faces. The special openings are called pits. The pits can feel heat. Pit vipers find their prey by sensing heat. They move their heads from side to side. They feel where heat is greatest. Heat coming directly from a warm body is greater than heat on the sides of a body.

Possible sample sentence write-outs may be

"I learned that a rattlesnake can feel heat with special pits on its face."

"I thought a rattlesnake found its prey by using its eyes, but now I know a rattlesnake finds its prey by using pits on its face, too."

"Did you know that a rattlesnake has special pits on its face to sense heat?"

"An interesting thing about a rattlesnake is that it can feel heat through special openings on its face called pits."

The Writing Link *(cont.)*

This type of exercise reinforces spelling and sentence structure. It also teaches a child responsibility—a child learns to go back to the story to check word spelling. It also provides elementary report writing skills. Students are taking information in a story source and reporting it in their own sentence construction.

The Questions

Five questions follow every story. Questions always contain one main idea, specific detail, and analogy question.

 ✱ The main idea question pushes a child to focus on the topic of what was read. It allows practice in discerning between answers that are too broad or too narrow.

 ✱ The specific detail question requires a child to retrieve or recall a particular fact mentioned in the story. Children gain practice referring back to a source. They also are pushed to think about the structure of the story. Where would this fact most likely be mentioned in the story? What paragraph would most likely contain the fact they are retrieving?

 ✱ The analogy question pushes a child to develop reasoning skills. It pairs two words mentioned in the story and asks the child to think about how the words relate to each other. A child is then asked to find an analogous pair. Children are expected to recognize and use analogies in all course readings, written work, and in listening. This particular type of question is found on many cognitive functioning tests.

 ✱ The remaining two questions are a mixture of vocabulary, inference, or extrapolation questions. Going back and reading the word in context can always answer vocabulary questions. The inference and extrapolation questions are the most difficult for many students, but they provide practice for what students will find on standardized tests. They also encourage a child to think beyond the story. They push a child to think critically about how facts can be interpreted or why something works.

The Test Link

Standardized tests have become obligatory in schools throughout our nation and the world. There are certain test taking skills and strategies that can be developed by using *Nonfiction Reading Comprehension: Science*.

 ✱ Questions can be answered on the page by circling the answer, or the questions can be answered by having students fill in the appropriate bubble pages on page 141. Filling in the bubble pages provides practice responding in a standardized test format.

 ✱ Questions are presented in a mixed up order, though the main idea question is always placed in the number one, two, or three slot. The analogy question is always placed in the three, four, or five slot. This mixed up order provides practice with standardized test formats. Athough reading comprehension passages often have main idea questions, the main idea question is not necessarily placed first.

The Test Link *(cont.)*

＊ A teacher may want to point out to students that often a main idea question can be used to help a child focus on what the story is about. A teacher may also want to point out that an analogy question can be done any time, as it is not crucial to the main focus of the story.

＊ A teacher may want to reinforce that a child should read every answer choice. Many children are afraid of not remembering information. Reinforcing this tip helps a child to remember that on multiple-choice tests, one is *identifying* the best answer, not making an answer up.

＊ A teacher may choose to discuss the strategy of eliminating wrong answer choices to find the correct one. Teachers should instruct children that even if they can only eliminate one answer choice, their guess would have a better chance of being right. A teacher may want to go through several questions to demonstrate this strategy. For example, in the *Snake Sense* selection, there is the question,

＊ What statement is true?
- ⓐ All snakes are pit vipers.
- ⓑ Some snakes are pit vipers.
- ⓒ All snakes are rattlesnakes.
- ⓓ Some snakes use their sense of sight to feel heat.

A child may know that there are many kinds of snakes in the world and that not all snakes are rattlesnakes. They may also know that the sense of sight is used to see, not to feel. Using prior knowledge, children may be able to eliminate choices C and D. At this point, a teacher can point out to children that one of the two remaining choices, either A or B, has a good chance of being right. A teacher can also instruct children that this is a good time to go back to the story and look for the paragraph where a pit viper is defined.

The Thrill of Science

The challenge in writing this book was to allow a child access to the thrills of science while understanding that many science words or concepts are beyond a child's elementary grade level. It is hoped that the range of stories and the ways concepts are presented reinforces basic science concepts, all while improving basic reading comprehension skills. It is also hoped that a child's imagination is whetted. After reading each story, a child will want to question and explore the subject.

Meeting Standards

Listed below are the McRel standards for language arts Level 2 (Grades 3–5).

McRel Standards are in **bold**. Benchmarks are in regular print. All lessons meet the following standards and benchmarks unless noted.

Uses stylistic and rhetorical aspects of writing.

- Uses a variety of sentence structures in writing (*All lessons where writing a complete sentence option is followed.*)
- Uses grammatical and mechanical conventions in written compositions

  Writes in cursive. (*All lessons where teacher follows the option of writing a sentence using a new word or completion of beginning sentence options in cursive.*)

  Uses conventions of spelling, capitalization, and punctuation in writing compositions. (*All lessons where teacher follows option of writing a sentence using a new word or completion of beginning sentence options.*)

Uses the general skills and strategies of the reading process.

- Previews text
- Establishes a purpose for reading
- Represents concrete information as explicit mental pictures
- Uses phonetic and structural analysis techniques, syntactic structure, and semantic context to decode unknown words
- Use a variety of context clues to decode unknown words
- Understands level-appropriate reading vocabulary
- Monitors own reading strategies and makes modifications as needed
- Adjust speed of reading to suit purpose and difficulty of material
- Understands the author's purpose

Uses reading skills and strategies to understand a variety of informational texts

- Summarizes and paraphrases information in texts
- Uses prior knowledge and experience to understand and respond to new information

Snake Sense

New words to practice.

Say each word ten times.

* rodent   * senses

* rattlesnake   * tongue

* prey   * jawbone

* viper   * vibrations

Choose one new word to write.

_____

- -

_____

Snake Sense

It is dark. There is no light. A small rodent tries to hide. It does not move. It is very quiet. Still, a rattlesnake can find the rodent's exact location. Even in the dark the rattlesnake will know exactly where to strike. How does the snake know where the rodent is? How can the snake find its prey in the dark?

Rattlesnakes are a type of pit viper. Pit vipers are snakes with special openings on their faces. The special openings are called pits. The pits can feel heat. Pit vipers find their prey by sensing heat. They move their heads from side to side. They feel where heat is greatest. Heat coming directly from a warm body is greater than heat on the sides of a body.

Rattlesnakes use their senses to find prey. They use different senses to find prey at different distances. Rattlesnakes use their sense of smell and sense of heat the most. They use these senses when their prey is close. They use their pits to sense heat, but what do they use to smell? Snakes use their tongues! A snake's tongue picks up smells from the air and ground. The tongue carries the smells into the snake's mouth. The smells are then "tasted" by a special organ. The organ is called Jacobsen's organ.

When prey is further away, rattlesnakes use their sense of sight. They have big eyes but no eyelids. This means that even when a rattlesnake is asleep, its eyes are open. The pupils in the eyes can open really wide. This lets in more light. This makes it so a snake can see even when the light is dim. Rattlesnakes can see prey up to 15 feet (4.6 meters) away.

For prey farthest away, a rattlesnake uses its sense of hearing. A rattlesnake has no ear openings. This is because the snake's ears are inside its head. So how does it hear? It uses its jawbone! The snake puts its jaws on the ground. It feels vibrations. It feels the ground move. The snake's jawbone carries the vibrations to the ear.

Snake Sense

After reading the story, answer the questions.
Fill in the circle next to the correct answer.

1. Why are a rattlesnake's eyes always open?

   ⓐ because a rattlesnake has no eyelids

   ⓑ so a rattlesnake can see prey up to 15 feet (4.6 meters) away

   ⓒ so a rattlesnake's pupils can open really wide in dim light

   ⓓ because a rattlesnake needs to find prey even when it is sleeping

2. This story is mainly about

   ⓐ pit vipers.

   ⓑ how a rattlesnake uses its tongue to smell.

   ⓒ why a rodent cannot hide from a rattlesnake.

   ⓓ how a rattlesnake uses its senses to find prey.

3. What sense would a rattlesnake probably use to find its prey if it were over 15 feet (4.6 meters) away?

   ⓐ sense of heat

   ⓑ sense of smell

   ⓒ sense of sight

   ⓓ sense of hearing

4. Think about how the word **pit** relates to **heat**. What words relate in the same way?

   | pit : heat |

   ⓐ eye : pupil

   ⓑ tongue : prey

   ⓒ jawbone : vibration

   ⓓ sense : Jacobson's organ

5. Which statement is true?

   ⓐ All snakes are pit vipers.

   ⓑ Some snakes are pit vipers.

   ⓒ All snakes are rattlesnakes.

   ⓓ Some snakes use their sense of sight to feel heat.

At the Top of Giants

New words to practice.

Say each word ten times.

* coast   * scientist

* redwood   * crown

* stories   * permit

* canopy   * salamander

Choose one new word to write.

_____

- -

_____

At the Top of Giants

Steve was dropping through the air. He was falling. He had to think fast. He reached out with one hand. He grabbed a branch. His shoulder was ripped from his socket, but he had stopped his fall.

Steve was able to get down safely, but what was Steve doing? Steve was in a giant coast redwood. Coast redwoods grow in Central and Northern California. Most trees are within 10 miles (16 kilometers) of the ocean. Scientists think some of the oldest coast redwoods are almost two thousand years old. The tallest ones are between 350 and 370 feet (107 to 113 meters) high. This is as high as a building with 35 to 37 stories!

Steve is a canopy scientist. He studies the canopies of coast redwood forests. Canopies are made up of tree crowns. The crown is the top branchy part of the tree. A coast redwood crown is very high. It is very hard to get to because the lowest branches can be 25 stories above the ground. Steve uses special ropes to climb the trees. He wears soft shoes so he does not hurt the tree. He has a special permit. The permit says Steve can climb the trees.

Steve and his students have found new things in the canopy. They found a new type of earthworm. They found a salamander. The salamander lives its entire life cycle above ground. They found plants that get their food and water from air and rain. They found bushes and shrubs growing in soil on the redwood. They found other types of trees growing high on the redwood, too. One spruce tree growing on the redwood was eight feet (2.4 meters) high!

Think about how tall the redwood tree is. How does the tree grow so tall? How does the tree move water through its giant trunk? Steve and other scientists are still learning. They are trying to find answers to their questions. One day you may be the one asking questions. Would you like to be high in a tree canopy while you look for answers?

At the Top of Giants

**After reading the story, answer the questions.
Fill in the circle next to the correct answer.**

1. This story is mainly about

   (a) scientists.

   (b) tree climbing.

   (c) coast redwoods.

   (d) plants and animals in trees.

2. What was special about the salamander?

   (a) It lived its entire life cycle above ground.

   (b) It could get its food and water from air and rain.

   (c) It ate a new type of earthworm that lived in the canopy.

   (d) It was found in a spruce tree growing in the redwood canopy.

3. Think about how the word **trunk** relates to **branch.** Which words relate in the same way?

trunk : branch

   (a) sun : ray

   (b) body : arm

   (c) tree : green

   (d) coast : ocean

4. Why does the author compare the size of the tree to how many stories there are in a building?

   (a) to help the reader understand how tall buildings are

   (b) to help the reader understand how tall the tree really is

   (c) to make the reader think about how wood from trees is used in buildings

   (d) to make the reader think about how far water from the ground has to travel to the canopy

5. What would you find above a tree canopy?

   (a) sky

   (b) more branches

   (c) new earthworms

   (d) small trees growing on big trees

Moon Tricks

New words to practice.

Say each word ten times.

* happened	* appearance
* disappear	* quarter
* visible	* cycle
* orbits	* phase

Choose one new word to write.

_____

- -

_____

Moon Tricks

Joy wanted to play a trick on Mrs. Blue, her teacher. Joy went to Mrs. Blue. She said, "Two weeks ago something happened. I lost my book. I left it outside on the porch. In the night I heard something. I looked out my window down at the porch. A big dog had my book in his mouth. He dragged it away. He made it disappear."

"I know this happened," said Joy. "I could see it all. I could see it all by the light of the moon. The moon was bright that night. It was as bright as the full moon was last night. The moonlight made everything visible." Mrs. Blue started to laugh. She knew that Joy was playing a trick on her. How did she know?

The moon orbits around our planet Earth. It circles the Earth. The moon's appearance changes as it completes its orbit. It appears to grow bigger and smaller. First, there is a new moon. The new moon is small. It grows into a first quarter moon. Then it gets even bigger. It grows into a full moon. The moon's appearance continues to change. The moon gets smaller. It goes from a full moon to a last quarter moon. Finally, it disappears. The entire cycle takes about a month.

The moon has no light of its own. The moon reflects light from the sun. The moon's appearance may change during the cycle, but the moon is always the same size. We see a new moon when the moon passes between the Earth and the Sun. We see a full moon when the sun and the moon are on opposite sides of the Earth.

Joy said that the full moon last night was as bright as the moon she saw two weeks ago. Remember that the moon cycle takes about four weeks. Each phase lasts about a week. Two weeks before a full moon, the moon would have been in the new moon phase. It would barely be visible! It could not have been as bright as a full moon!

Moon Tricks

After reading the story, answer the questions.
Fill in the circle next to the correct answer.

1. How did the author let you know that Mrs. Blue wasn't mad at Joy for trying to trick her?

   ⓐ Mrs. Blue started to laugh.

   ⓑ Mrs. Blue knew about the moon.

   ⓒ Mrs. Blue didn't ask Joy to pay for the book.

   ⓓ Mrs. Blue wanted Joy to learn the moon phases.

2. This story is mainly about

   ⓐ Joy and the dog.

   ⓑ the moon and its orbit.

   ⓒ the full moon.

   ⓓ Joy's trick and how Mrs. Blue knew.

3. What do we see when the sun and the moon are on opposite sides of the Earth?

   ⓐ a new moon

   ⓑ a full moon

   ⓒ a last quarter moon

   ⓓ a first quarter moon

4. When the moon completes its cycle,

   ⓐ about a week's time has passed.

   ⓑ the sun has reflected its light.

   ⓒ the size of the moon has changed.

   ⓓ it has completed its orbit around the Earth.

5. Think about how the word **Moon** relates to **Earth**. Which words relate in the same way?

Moon : Earth

   ⓐ Earth : Sun

   ⓑ Sun : reflect

   ⓒ orbit : cycle

   ⓓ planet : Earth

Not Nice Lice

New words to practice.
Say each word ten times.

✳ lice	✳ polite
✳ parasites	✳ louse
✳ archeologists	✳ stylets
✳ mummified	✳ scalp

Choose one new word to write.

Not Nice Lice

It is not nice when you have lice. Lice are parasites. Parasites do not go out and get their own food. Parasites eat what they live on. Lice live on your head. They make their home in your hair. You are their host. Parasites eat their hosts. Lice suck your blood.

Lice have been around a long time. Archeologists study how people lived long ago. Archeologists have found mummified lice! They found the mummified lice in ancient tombs in Egypt! George Washington wrote a book about manners. He wrote that it was not polite to kill your own lice when people were watching. If you saw a louse on someone else, it was polite to brush it away for him or her.

A louse has three pointy tubes in its mouth. The pointy tubes are called stylets. To drink blood, a louse pushes its stylets into its host's head. The stylets are small so it does not hurt. Lice use their stylets like straws. After they drink, lice spit. They spit into the holes that they made. The spit keeps the blood from making a scab.

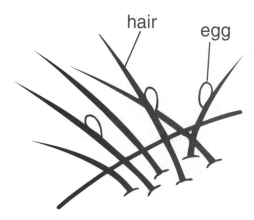

hair   egg

The spit makes you itch. This makes many people scratch. Often, if you scratch a lot, you will bleed more. Lice like this. The blood gives a louse a free meal. It gets to eat without having to work. If you get lice, you have to use a special shampoo. You have to wash your scalp and hair with the shampoo. You have to use a special comb to comb out lice eggs. The eggs are hard to comb out. They are glued to the hair.

Lice cannot fly or jump. How do you get lice? You do not get lice because you are dirty. In fact, lice like a clean scalp. Lice will crawl into any hair they come into contact with. You can get lice when your head touches someone else's. You can get lice from using someone else's comb or brush. You can get lice from wearing someone else's hat.

Not Nice Lice

**After reading the story, answer the questions.
Fill in the circle next to the correct answer.**

1. This story is mainly about

   ⓐ sucking blood.

   ⓑ a louse's host.

   ⓒ one kind of parasite.

   ⓓ how to be polite with lice.

2. How many stylets does a louse have?

   ⓐ one

   ⓑ two

   ⓒ three

   ⓓ four

3. How do you get lice?

   ⓐ by lice flying onto your head

   ⓑ by lice jumping onto your scalp

   ⓒ by lice laying eggs on your hair

   ⓓ by lice coming into contact with you

4. From what George Washington wrote, you can tell that

   ⓐ few people probably host parasites.

   ⓑ lice are probably common parasites.

   ⓒ probably people long ago were not polite.

   ⓓ probably people long ago were very polite.

5. Think about how the word **louse** relates to **lice.** Which words relate in the same way?

   | louse : lice |

   ⓐ feet : foot

   ⓑ mouse : mice

   ⓒ goose : geese

   ⓓ house : houses

Seeing Colors at Night

New words to practice.

Say each word ten times.

* source   * iris

* sensitive   * pupil

* image   * adapted

* dim   * compound

Choose one new word to write.

_____

- -

_____

Seeing Colors at Night

You can see colors during the day. Why can't you see colors at night? You need light to see. Light comes from many different sources. The sun and moon are light sources. An electric bulb is a source, too. When light hits an object, light waves bounce off. The light is reflected. You have special light-sensitive cells in your eyes. These special cells sense the light. They send signals to your brain.

You have a lot of light-sensitive cells. You have well over one million! You have two types of light-sensitive cells. You have rod cells and cone cells. The cells get their names from the way they are shaped. Rod cells are used to see in black and white. Rod cells make a black and white image or picture. They only need a little light to work. You have a lot more rod cells than cone cells.

Cone cells let us see color. Cone cells make a colored image. They need a lot of light to work. Think about sunlight. Think about light from the moon. Sunlight is bright. Moonlight is dim. Our color-sensitive cone cells do not respond to the dim moonlight. There is not enough light.

The iris is the part of the eye that gives it its color. Your pupil looks like a black dot. It is in the center of your iris. The pupil is a small opening. Muscles in the iris control the amount of light passing through the pupil. The muscles make the pupil bigger and smaller. In dim light, your pupils open wide. Your eye wants to let in as much light as possible. In bright light, your pupils get smaller.

All eyes are not the same. One type of fish swims at the surface of the water. The top half of the fish eye is adapted to seeing in air. The bottom half is adapted to seeing in water. Flies have compound eyes. Compound eyes are made up of many little eyes joined together. All the eyes point in different directions. This lets a fly see all around it at the same time.

Seeing Colors at Night

After reading the story, answer the questions.
Fill in the circle next to the correct answer.

1. This story is mainly about
   - ⓐ rod cells.
   - ⓑ how our eyes respond to light.
   - ⓒ how all eyes are not the same.
   - ⓓ bright sunlight and dim moonlight.

2. What part of the eye needs a lot of light to work?
   - ⓐ the iris
   - ⓑ the pupil
   - ⓒ the rod cells
   - ⓓ the cone cells

3. It is a very bright, sunny day. You were outside. You just went inside. Your pupils would
   - ⓐ become compound.
   - ⓑ stay the same size.
   - ⓒ start to get bigger.
   - ⓓ start to get smaller.

4. A dog's ear can hear high sounds we cannot hear. You could say that a dog's ear is more
   - ⓐ compound than ours.
   - ⓑ an image than ours.
   - ⓒ reflected than ours.
   - ⓓ sensitive than ours.

5. Think about how the word **bright** relates to **dim.** Which words relate in the same way?

bright : dim

   - ⓐ hard : soft
   - ⓑ ligh t: sun
   - ⓒ big : bigger
   - ⓓ fish : water

Adding Up an Elephant

New words to practice.

Say each word ten times.

✳ observation	✳ exactly
✳ data	✳ touched
✳ enough	✳ decided
✳ collect	✳ argued

Choose one new word to write.

_____

- - - - - - - - - - - - - - - - - - - -

_____

Adding Up an Elephant

There are a lot of stories. Some stories are written to teach us lessons. The story that follows is a very old story. It teaches us a lesson. The lesson is about making observations. It is about collecting data. It teaches us that often one observation is not enough. It teaches us that we have to be careful about how we collect data.

Six blind men heard about a new animal. The animal was called an elephant. They wanted to know what an elephant was like. The blind men walked in a line. They walked to where the elephant was. The elephant's keeper told the blind men they could feel the elephant. The first man felt the side of the elephant. He said, "It is big. It is smooth. I know exactly what an elephant is like. An elephant is like a big, smooth wall."

The second man touched the elephant's trunk. The second man said, "It is round. It is long. An elephant is like a round, long snake." The third man touched the elephant's tusk. He cried out in pain. He decided that an elephant was like a sharp spear.

The fourth man felt the elephant's leg. He decided that an elephant was like a tall tree. The fifth man touched the elephant's ear. He decided that that an elephant was like a wide fan. The sixth man touched the tail of the elephant. He said, "It is thin. It is strong. I know exactly what an elephant is like. An elephant is like a thin, strong rope."

After they sat down, the blind men began to argue. Was an elephant like a big, smooth wall or a round, long snake? Was it like a sharp spear or a tall tree? Was it like a wide fan or a thin, strong rope? The men argued and argued. The keeper heard the men arguing. He told the men that they needed to collect more data. One observation each was not enough. They would find that an elephant was all of those things added together.

Adding Up an Elephant

After reading the story, answer the questions.
Fill in the circle next to the correct answer.

1. What blind man decided that an elephant was like a sharp spear?

   (a) first
   (b) third
   (c) fifth
   (d) sixth

2. If someone wanted to collect data about you

   (a) many observations over time would be needed.
   (b) they would only need to ask you for the data.
   (c) one observation during the day would be enough.
   (d) you would have to find an elephant that you could touch.

3. This story is mainly about

   (a) adding.
   (b) elephants.
   (c) being blind.
   (d) making observations.

4. What lesson did the old story teach?

   (a) that often data is wrong
   (b) that we have to be careful
   (c) that an elephant is like many things
   (d) that often one observation is not enough

5. Think about how the word **blind** relates to **see.** Which words relate in the same way?

   | blind : see |

   (a) deaf : hear
   (b) sleepy : nap
   (c) happy : smile
   (d) strong : swim

A 200,000 Year-Old Meal

New words to practice.
Say each word ten times.

* backhoe

* excavating

* exposed

* unusual

* bison

* roamed

* shriveled

* bulky

Choose one new word to write.

_____

- - - - - - - - - - - - - - - - - -

_____

A 200,000 Year-Old Meal

One day Jim was using a backhoe. A backhoe is a machine. It is used for excavating dirt. When something is excavated, it is dug out. It is removed. Jim was a gold miner. He was in Canada. Jim's excavating exposed something unusual. When something is exposed, it can be seen. Jim's excavating exposed an animal. It exposed a bison.

Bison are big, cow-like animals. They have horns. Long ago, they roamed across North America. They roamed across parts of Europe, too. They roamed in big groups, or herds. They roamed on treeless plains. They ate grass. There are some bison alive today. The American bison is also known as a buffalo.

Jim's bison was frozen. It was like a mummy. It had shriveled up. Jim's daughter knew scientists might want the bison. She bagged it up. She put it in a freezer. There was a problem. The bison was bulky. It took up too much space. It was hard to handle. So Jim's daughter moved the bulky mass outside. It was very cold outside. She knew the bison would stay frozen.

A pack of wolves found the bison. The wolves were hungry. The pack of wolves tore through the plastic. The wolves chewed the shriveled bison to bits. Scientists still wanted the bison. They did tests on what the wolves left. They looked at the age of the ice the bison was found in. The scientists found that the bison was the oldest bison ever found in North America. The bison was 200,000 years old!

How did the wolves find the bison? They found it by its smell. They were able to eat it. This meant that it was not rotten. The meat was not spoiled. It was still fresh. This was very unusual. It was a very rare find. Scientists could have learned a lot from the bison meat. They could have learned how some animals from long ago are like some animals today. Instead, a pack of wolves ate a meal that was 200,000 years old!

A 200,000 Year-Old Meal

After reading the story, answer the questions.
Fill in the circle next to the correct answer.

1. This story is mainly about

   ⓐ fresh meat.

   ⓑ an unusual find.

   ⓒ what wolves eat.

   ⓓ a gold miner named Jim.

2. What made the bison Jim found rare and unusual?

   ⓐ Wolves ate it.

   ⓑ It was very old.

   ⓒ It was like a mummy.

   ⓓ The meat was not spoiled.

3. What does the word roam mean?

   ⓐ to move and eat grass

   ⓑ to travel in a large group

   ⓒ to wander and travel about

   ⓓ to live on a treeless plain

4. Where would someone most likely expose a bison like the one Jim did?

   ⓐ where it is very hot

   ⓑ where it is very wet

   ⓒ where it is very dry

   ⓓ where it is very cold

5. Think about how the word **herd** relates to **bison**. Which words relate in the same way?

   > **herd : bison**

   ⓐ cat : kittens

   ⓑ pack : wolves

   ⓒ plains : trees

   ⓓ unusual : rare

A Riddle

New words to practice.
Say each word ten times.

✳ prevent	✳ materials
✳ through	✳ sundials
✳ enormous	✳ rovers
✳ opaque	✳ hours

Choose one new word to write.

_____

- -

_____

A Riddle

It is yours. You cannot give it away. You cannot lend it. Someone cannot give it to you. It is sometimes smaller than you. It is sometimes bigger than you. Sometimes, you do not even have it! What can it be? The answer is—your shadow!

When do shadows form? Shadows form when light hits an object that will not let light through it. The shadow forms behind the object. The shadow is in the same shape as the object. This is because light rays only travel in straight lines. Light rays cannot bend around an object. If you are near a light, you prevent a lot of light from getting through. Your shadow is big. If you are farther away, you block less light. You have a smaller shadow.

You are in an enormous shadow every day. You cannot get away from it. What makes this enormous shadow? The sun shines on one side of the earth. The earth is opaque. Objects or materials that can block out light are called opaque. Opaque materials block light rays. The earth prevents or blocks the sun's rays from getting through. One side of the earth faces the sun. The other side of the earth is in shadow. The shadow makes the night.

Why are some shadows darker than others? Some objects block more light than others. They are more opaque. A book does not let light through it. It is opaque. A book's shadow will be dark. A piece of paper lets more light through than a book. It is not as opaque. The paper's shadow will be lighter than the book's.

Long ago, people used shadows to tell time. They would put down a post. They would watch its shadow. The shadow moved as the sun moved across the sky. These types of clocks were called sundials. We sent rovers to Mars. The rovers were machines that traveled across the surface of Mars. The rovers had special sundials on them. Mars has longer hours than on Earth. The sundials were made so that they would show Mars' longer hours!

A Riddle

**After reading the story, answer the questions.
Fill in the circle next to the correct answer.**

1. Put your hand close to a light. The shadow of your hand would be

   ⓐ the same as your hand far away.

   ⓑ darker than if your hand were far away.

   ⓒ bigger than if your hand were far away.

   ⓓ smaller than if your hand were far away.

2. What object would likely be the most opaque?

   ⓐ a brick

   ⓑ a glass

   ⓒ a tree leaf

   ⓓ a light shirt

3. This story is mainly about

   ⓐ shadows.

   ⓑ riddles.

   ⓒ the size of shadows.

   ⓓ how to tell time with shadows.

4. Why does an object's shadow have the same shape as the object?

   ⓐ Light rays can bend.

   ⓑ Light rays travel in straight lines.

   ⓒ The object's shadow is not as opaque as the object.

   ⓓ The object blocks a lot of light from getting through.

5. Think about how the word **light** relates to **shadow**. Which words relate in the same way?

   | light : shadow |

   ⓐ bike : ride

   ⓑ ant : honey

   ⓒ dark : Earth

   ⓓ cloth : pants

All About Air

New words to practice.
Say each word ten times.

✳ particles	✳ weigh
✳ atoms	✳ pressure
✳ spread	✳ barometer
✳ oxygen	✳ temperature

Choose one new word to write.

_____

- -

_____

All About Air

Air is all around us. Air is a mixture of gases. It is made up of tiny particles we cannot see. The particles are atoms. Everything in the world is made up of atoms. The atoms in gases can spread out. They can spread out to take the shape of any space. One of the gases in air is oxygen. We need oxygen to breathe.

Some people think air does not weigh anything. Air is light, but it does weigh something. A roomful of air weighs about as much as a person. We call the weight of all the air in the sky pushing down on Earth air pressure. Air pressure is greatest down by the ocean or other low land. Air pressure is less high in the mountains. This is because there is less air high up.

Everest is the tallest mountain in the world. There is very little air on the top of Everest. Climbers use bottled oxygen to help breathe at the top of Everest. A helicopter could not take off on the top of Everest. There is not enough air.

We use a barometer to measure air pressure. The barometer tells us if the air pressure is high or low. We look at a barometer to predict the weather. When the air pressure is high, the weather is often sunny. This is because it is hard for clouds to form. The air is too heavy! When the air pressure is low, it is easy for clouds to form. When the air pressure is low, it often rains.

Air pressure can change the way we cook. Water boils at 212 F° or 100 C° at sea level. Go high up on a mountain. The air pressure is less. It takes less energy to boil the water. Water will boil at a lower temperature! You can still cook your food when the air pressure is less, but you will have to cook it longer. You will have to cook it longer because the water boils at a lower temperature.

All About Air

After reading the story, answer the questions.
Fill in the circle next to the correct answer.

1. The tiny particles in air

   ⓐ are atoms.

   ⓑ can be seen.

   ⓒ are only in air.

   ⓓ cannot spread out.

2. If a barometer showed that the air pressure was falling and getting low, one might soon see

   ⓐ hot weather.

   ⓑ cold weather.

   ⓒ sunny weather.

   ⓓ rainy weather.

3. This story is mainly about

   ⓐ atoms and air.

   ⓑ oxygen and gases.

   ⓒ barometers and rain.

   ⓓ air and air pressure.

4. From the story, you can tell that one atom

   ⓐ weighs a lot.

   ⓑ weighs very little.

   ⓒ weighs more than a person.

   ⓓ weighs less high on a mountain top.

5. Think about how the word **barometer** relates to **pressure**. Which words relate in the same way?

   | barometer : pressure |

   ⓐ day : week

   ⓑ rain : cloud

   ⓒ clock : time

   ⓓ mountain : weigh

Burning Ships

New words to practice.

Say each word ten times.

✳ enemy	✳ focal point
✳ harbor	✳ temperature
✳ archer	✳ concave
✳ concentrate	✳ reflected

Choose one new word to write.

_____

- -

_____

Burning Ships Story

Long ago, enemy ships entered a harbor. The enemy ships were from Rome. The harbor was on the island of Sicily. The enemy ships had come to attack the people of Sicily. This was more than 2,000 years ago. It is said that all of a sudden the enemy ships burst into flames. The ships were out in the water. They were out of range of archers. Archers use bows. They shoot arrows with their bows. The archer's arrows could not reach the ships. The ships were too far away. So why did they burst into flames? What was going on?

Light comes from the sun. Light travels in rays. The rays are straight. They do not bend around corners. You can concentrate the sun's light. When something is concentrated, things are brought close together. They are made stronger or thicker. It is focused. You can concentrate the sun's light with a lens. A lens has curved sides. The sides are smooth.

A lens brings rays of sunlight to a "focal point." All the energy of the light is concentrated into this point. The temperature at the focal point will rise. It will get very hot. It can even catch on fire.

You can concentrate the sun's light with a mirror, too. The story goes that a man named Archimedes set the ships on fire. Archimedes was very good at math. He made many machines. To set the ships on fire, Archimedes made a "burning mirror." The mirror was concave. When something is concave, it is shaped like a dish. It is hollow and rounded like the inside of a bowl. It has curved, smooth sides.

A mirror has a smooth, shiny surface. A mirror reflects light. When light is reflected, the light rays bounce back. Light rays were reflected off of Archimedes' mirror. Because the mirror was concave, the light was reflected a certain way. It concentrated the light. Archimedes directed the light at the enemy ships. The focal point of the light was very hot. The high temperature made the ships burst into flames.

Burning Ships

After reading the story, answer the questions.
Fill in the circle next to the correct answer.

1. When light rays bounce back they are

   ⓐ concave.

   ⓑ straight.

   ⓒ reflected.

   ⓓ concentrated.

2. How might a fire start?

   ⓐ Someone drops a paper. The paper acts as a lens.

   ⓑ Someone shoots an arrow. The arrow acts as a lens.

   ⓒ Someone drops a bottle. The bottle acts as a lens.

   ⓓ Someone spills a drink. The spilled drink acts as a lens.

3. This story is mainly about

   ⓐ light.

   ⓑ Archimedes.

   ⓒ burning ships.

   ⓓ what concentrated light can do.

4. What was true of Archimedes' mirror?

   ⓐ It was concave.

   ⓑ Its surface was not smooth.

   ⓒ It did not concentrate light.

   ⓓ It was out of the range of the archers.

5. Think about how the word **enemy** relates to **friend.** Which words relate in the same way?

enemy : friend

   ⓐ hate : like

   ⓑ smile : grin

   ⓒ concentrate : lens

   ⓓ temperature : rise

A True Life Mystery

New words to practice.

Say each word ten times.

* species   * disease

* extinct   * solved

* mystery   * predator

* pesticides   * nocturnal

Choose one new word to write.

_____

- - - - - - - - - - - - - - - - - -

_____

A True Life Mystery

The sun rose to shine warmly on the forest. The dark, lush forest was in Guam. Guam is an island in the Pacific Ocean. On any other island, one would hear the sound of birds greeting the morning sun. No birds sang on Guam. Many birds used to sing on Guam. Their songs and cries would ring through the forests. Now there was silence.

Scientists were seeing bird species on Guam becoming extinct. When something becomes extinct, it is no longer living. Bird species on Guam were becoming extinct fast. Would the scientists figure out why? Would the scientists be able to stop it before it was too late? Some birds were caught in special nets. They were taken to zoos in other countries. The zoos would keep the birds safe. They would try to raise more birds in the zoo. Then, when it was safe, they could take the birds back to Guam.

A student named Julie came to solve the mystery. She looked at pesticides. Pesticides are used to kill pests. Pesticides can be sprayed on plants and insects. It was not the pesticides. Was it a disease? Julie brought birds to the island. She put them outside. She tested their blood. The birds did not get sick. It was not a disease. Finally Julie solved the mystery.

During World War II, a snake caught a ride on a boat. It came from the Philippines. It got loose on the island. The snake had no natural predators on the island. The snake was nocturnal. It was awake at night. It was a nocturnal predator. The snake laid eggs and more snakes were born. The snakes bit babies. They ate chickens. They ate birds and bird eggs. The snakes could climb power cables, too. They caused the power to go out nearly 1,000 times between 1978 and 1990.

The mystery is solved, but the work is not over. Today scientists are working on keeping the last birds safe from snakes. They are working hard at bringing back birds to Guam. They are trying to stop snakes from going to other islands, too.

A True Life Mystery

After reading the story, answer the questions.
Fill in the circle next to the correct answer.

1. This story is mainly about

   ⓐ snakes.

   ⓑ extinct birds.

   ⓒ a bird mystery.

   ⓓ the island of Guam.

2. A nocturnal predator

   ⓐ moves at night.

   ⓑ hunts at night.

   ⓒ moves during the day.

   ⓓ hunts during the day.

3. Why were some birds caught and sent to zoos?

   ⓐ So scientists could keep them safe.

   ⓑ So scientists could see if they had a disease.

   ⓒ So scientists could see if pesticides were killing them.

   ⓓ So scientists could see if they could raise more birds for other zoos.

4. Think about how the word **bird** relates to **song**. Which words relate in the same way?

bird : song

   ⓐ meow : cat

   ⓑ dog : bark

   ⓒ island : Guam

   ⓓ snake : predator

5. What was one reason the snake did so well on Guam?

   ⓐ It hunted during the day.

   ⓑ Pesticides couldn't kill it.

   ⓒ It had no natural predators.

   ⓓ It was not tired from swimming.

Hunter in the Night Sky

New words to practice.
Say each word ten times.

* mighty   * astronomers

* recognize   * different

* groups   * Egypt

* constellations   * placed

Choose one new word to write.

_____

- -

_____

Hunter in the Night Sky

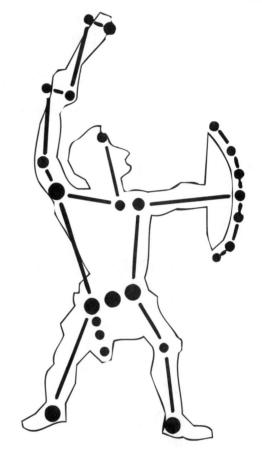

Look in the sky. You will see a mighty hunter. The mighty hunter is Orion. He is easy to find. He has a bright belt. The belt is made of three bright stars. The stars are all in a line. Why do people look for the mighty hunter? How did he get there? What is the story written up there in the sky?

People have been watching the stars since long ago. They saw that stars move in set patterns across the sky. They learned to recognize groups of stars. They gave names to the groups of stars. These groups of stars are called constellations. Astronomers mapped the first constellations 5,000 years ago. Today, we recognize 88 constellations.

The astronomers made star maps. The maps helped people to remember where and when they would see the stars. They saw that stars seemed to move from east to west. The stars are not moving. The Earth spins from west to east. The turning Earth makes the stars look like they are moving. We see different constellations in different seasons. We see some constellations in the winter. We see different constellations in the summer.

Long ago, the constellations helped people know what time it was. For example, people in Egypt looked for the constellation Canis Major. Canis Major is the Great Dog. When people saw the Great Dog, they knew the Nile River would soon flood. The brightest star in the entire sky is Sirius. Sirius makes up part of the Great Dog. Sirius is known as the Dog Star. Other constellations told the people in Egypt when it was time to harvest their crops.

There are stories about Canis Major in old Greek myths. The myths say that Orion's friend was tricked. Orion's friend was tricked into shooting Orion. His friend was very sad when she found out what she had done. She placed Orion in the sky forever. Orion had two hunting dogs. The Great Dog was one of them. Orion's friend put the dogs in the sky, too. She placed them so they could follow their master's heels.

Hunter in the Night Sky

**After reading the story, answer the questions.
Fill in the circle next to the correct answer.**

1. This story is mainly about

   ⓐ stars.

   ⓑ astronomers.

   ⓒ the Great Dog.

   ⓓ constellations.

2. What did people know long ago in Egypt when they saw the constellation Canis Major?

   ⓐ that the stars were moving

   ⓑ that the Nile River would soon flood

   ⓒ that Orion's friend had been tricked

   ⓓ that it was time to harvest their crops

3. Think about how the word **constellation** relates to **stars.** Which words relate in the same way?

constellation : stars

   ⓐ dog : puppy

   ⓑ paper : books

   ⓒ forest : trees

   ⓓ child : schools

4. An astronomer is someone

   ⓐ who was tricked.

   ⓑ who studies stars.

   ⓒ who studies myths.

   ⓓ who is from Egypt.

5. If you saw Orion in winter, it is likely that

   ⓐ you would not see Orion in the summer.

   ⓑ you would be able to see Orion in all the seasons.

   ⓒ you would not be able to see Sirius, the Dog Star.

   ⓓ you would not be able to see the constellation the Great Dog.

Strange Partners

New words to practice.

Say each word ten times.

* guide   * symbiosis

* strange   * organisms

* partners   * relationship

* survive   * protect

Choose one new word to write.

_____

- -

_____

Strange Partners

You know about seeing-eye dogs. They help guide people who cannot see. Do you know about seeing-eye fish? There is a type of shrimp that is blind. It cannot see at all. The shrimp survives by using a seeing-eye fish. The shrimp partners with a goby fish. The shrimp and the fish may seem like strange partners, but they help each other to survive.

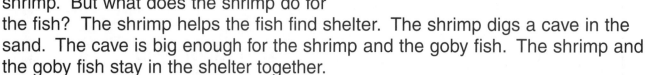

When the shrimp wants to search for food, it taps on the goby fish. The shrimp grabs its partner with its claw. The fish guides the shrimp. But what does the shrimp do for the fish? The shrimp helps the fish find shelter. The shrimp digs a cave in the sand. The cave is big enough for the shrimp and the goby fish. The shrimp and the goby fish stay in the shelter together.

What do scientists call these strange partnerships? Scientists call these strange partnerships symbiosis. Symbiosis is a partnership between two organisms. In some symbiotic relationships, both organisms are helped. Both the blind shrimp and the goby fish are helped. In another symbiotic relationship, a plant and an ant help one another.

The acacia plant has big thorns. The big thorns cover the plant. The thorns stop small animals from eating the plant. But they do not stop the big animals. This is where the ants come in. The ants protect the plant from big animals. How do the ants protect the plant? When a big animal bites the plant, the ants rush out. They attack the animal. They bite its nose! The ants make the animal leave.

Why do the ants protect the acacia plant? The plant provides shelter and food for the ants. The plant makes special nectar. The nectar smells very good to the ants. Ants eat the nectar. It is all they need to eat. Ants may spend their entire lives on the plant. They do not need to go anywhere else to survive. They will attack any big animal that may hurt their home.

Strange Partners

After reading the story, answer the questions.
Fill in the circle next to the correct answer.

1. This story is mainly about
   - (a) two examples of symbiosis.
   - (b) two types of relationships.
   - (c) how ants attack big animals.
   - (d) how blind shrimp and fish are partners.

2. Why does the tree need the ants?
   - (a) to eat the nectar
   - (b) to provide shelter
   - (c) to attack the big animals that can eat the thorns
   - (d) to attack the small animals that can eat the thorns

3. If you need someone to show you where something is or how to do something, you might need a
   - (a) guide.
   - (b) partner.
   - (c) organism.
   - (d) relationship.

4. What might be an example of a symbiotic relationship?
   - (a) a cow and the grass it eats
   - (b) a shark and the fish it eats
   - (c) a bee and the honey it makes
   - (d) a crab and the animals that live on its back

5. Think about how the word **eye** relates to **see.** Which words relate in the same way?

eye : see

   - (a) tree : animal
   - (b) thorn : protect
   - (c) organism : partner
   - (d) relationship : shrimp

Warts

New words to practice.
Say each word ten times.

* virus   * host

* causes   * reproduce

* electron   * bulge

* microscope   * contagious

Choose one new word to write.

_____

- - - - - - - - - - - - - - - - - - - -

_____

Warts

What do the common cold and warts have in common? A virus causes the common cold. A virus causes warts. There are many viruses in the world. They affect living things in different ways. The virus that causes warts in humans is caused by the *papilloma* virus. It is not the same virus that causes the common cold.

Viruses are tiny. You can only see them with an electron microscope. Electron microscopes are very powerful. With an electron microscope, you can see that the *papilloma* virus has 72 sides. It looks a bit like a soccer ball. Viruses use host cells to reproduce. They use host cells to make new viruses. The host cells for the *papilloma* virus need to be skin cells. They need to be human.

How does the virus get inside its host? The virus sits on your body. It waits for a break. It enters your body through a cut or crack. It attaches itself to a skin cell. The virus still needs to get inside the cell. Think about a lock. A lock needs a special key to open it. Skin cells have parts that act like locks. They do not open up unless a special key fits.

The virus plays a trick on the cell. It has a part shaped like the special key! Once the virus gets in, it takes over. It uses the cell to reproduce new viruses. It uses the cell to make billions and billions of new viruses. The skin cells fill up. They swell. They bulge out. They form a wart.

Wart viruses are contagious. When something is contagious, it is easily spread. We leave tiny bits of dead skin all around us. It rubs off on things we touch. If we have warts, we leave a trail of wart viruses. Warts bulge out. The viruses rub off the bulging warts. About one in eight children get warts. Most warts go away by themselves. Sometimes a doctor removes warts. The doctor freezes it or cuts it out. Sometimes the doctor zaps it with a laser beam.

Warts

After reading the story, answer the questions.
Fill in the circle next to the correct answer.

1. This story is mainly about

ⓐ the papilloma virus.

ⓑ how a doctor can remove a wart.

ⓒ the way a virus plays a trick on a cell.

ⓓ how the common cold and warts are the same.

2. A flea lives on a dog. The dog is

ⓐ a cell.

ⓑ a host.

ⓒ a virus.

ⓓ a bulge.

3. Think about how the word **small** relates to **tiny**. Which words relate in the same way?

small : tiny

ⓐ rub : trail

ⓑ freeze : cut

ⓒ microscope : see

ⓓ strong : powerful

4. One way to avoid or not get warts is to

ⓐ wash and cover your cuts.

ⓑ wear other people's dirty clothes.

ⓒ use the same towel as other people.

ⓓ go barefoot where other people go barefoot.

5. What does the papilloma virus look like?

ⓐ a lock

ⓑ a soccer ball

ⓒ a special key

ⓓ a common cold virus

The Fastest Thing in the Universe

New words to practice.

Say each word ten times.

* travels

* universe

* incredible

* energy

* receive

* renewable

* expensive

* solar-powered

Choose one new word to write.

_____

- -

_____

The Fastest Thing in the Universe

Something travels fast. It travels faster than anything else in the universe. What is it? The answer is light. Light travels faster than anything else in the universe. How fast is fast? Light travels at the incredible speed of 186,281 miles (300,000 kilometers) per second!

The Sun gives off energy. The energy is in the form of heat and light. The Sun is very far away. Still, we receive energy from the Sun. We receive it fast. How long does it take for the Sun's light to reach us? It takes about eight minutes. We need energy from the Sun. We could not live on Earth without it.

Light from the Sun warms us. It warms the land and the seas. It lights up the sky. We use its energy to grow. What is one way we do this? Think of plants. Plants use the energy of sunlight to make food. They change the Sun's energy to another form. They store the Sun's energy. Anything that eats the plant is getting some of the Sun's energy. We eat plants. We eat animals that eat plants, too. We are getting the Sun's energy from what we eat.

The Sun is very big. It is so big that more than a million Earth's could fit inside it. Only a tiny bit of the Sun's energy reaches the earth. Still, it is an incredible amount. How much is it? Every fifteen minutes the Earth receives enough energy to power everything on our planet for a whole year! Energy from the sun is renewable. It will never run out.

So why don't we use the Sun's energy to heat our houses? Why don't we use this form of renewable energy to drive our cars? It is expensive. It is expensive to make electricity from sunlight. Scientists are working hard. They are working to find a good, cheap way. We sent a probe to Mars. The probe landed on Mars. It rolled across the Red Planet. The probe was solar-powered! Perhaps one day all of the cars on Earth will be solar-powered, too!

The Fastest Thing in the Universe

After reading the story, answer the questions.
Fill in the circle next to the correct answer.

1. Why don't we make all of our electricity from sunlight?

   ⓐ We do not know how.

   ⓑ It is too expensive.

   ⓒ It is not renewable.

   ⓓ Scientists are not working on this.

2. This story is mainly about

   ⓐ the speed of light.

   ⓑ how much energy we get from the sun.

   ⓒ how energy from the sun is renewable.

   ⓓ light from the sun and how it is used.

3. Could you ever blow out a candle and jump into bed before it gets dark?

   ⓐ No because you cannot move faster than light.

   ⓑ Yes because the candle's light is not from the sun.

   ⓒ No because the candle's light is not as big as the sun.

   ⓓ Yes because if you jump, you can move faster than light.

4. Think about how the word **store** relates to **hold.** Which words relate in the same way?

store : hold

   ⓐ spend : use

   ⓑ sun : renewable

   ⓒ energy : sunlight

   ⓓ expensive : probe

5. When something is renewable it means

   ⓐ that it is expensive.

   ⓑ that you can keep on making more of it.

   ⓒ that it can be changed to another form.

   ⓓ that you will run out when you use it up.

Turtle or Tortoise

New words to practice.
Say each word ten times.

* tortoise   * appeared

* turtle   * predator

* domed   * skeleton

* primitive   * detective

Choose one new word to write.

_____

- -

_____

Turtle or Tortoise

Is a tortoise a turtle? Yes, a tortoise is a turtle. There are over 200 different kinds of turtles. They fall into three groups. There are freshwater turtles. There are sea turtles. There are tortoises. Tortoises live on dry land. All turtles have shells on their backs. The shells of most tortoises look different than other turtles. This is because the tortoise does not have a flat shell. A tortoise's shell is domed. When something is domed, it is round. It is like half of a ball.

Turtles are like dinosaurs. They are primitive reptiles. A reptile is not a mammal. A reptile is cold-blooded. It lays eggs. When something is primitive, it is ancient. It is living in earlier times. Turtles first appeared on Earth about 200 million years ago. The dinosaurs are gone, but the turtles are still plodding along.

When the turtles first appeared, they had smaller shells. Over time, they grew larger shells. The larger shells helped protect them from predators. The shells grew big enough for the turtles to fit their heads inside. This helped to keep them safe from predators. A turtle's shell is part of its skeleton. You can't remove it. You can't take off a skeleton! The shell is made of flat, bony plates. The plates are attached to the turtle's ribs and backbone.

Think for a moment like a detective. Think about tortoise legs. They are thick and heavy. They are not slim and flat. They do not have webbed toes. They are not for swimming. Think about how slowly a tortoise walks. To go just one mile (1.6 kilometers), it takes a tortoise five hours! Now, be a detective. What can a tortoise eat? Can it be something that can run away?

A tortoise eats plants. Some tortoises grow very big. They can weigh over 600 pounds (272 kilograms). They have to eat lots of plants to grow that big. Good thing plants can't run away! Tortoises can get their water from plants they eat. In the desert, they eat cactus and other plants that store water.

Turtle or Tortoise

**After reading the story, answer the questions.
Fill in the circle next to the correct answer.**

1. What statement is true?

   (a) All turtles are tortoises.

   (b) All tortoises are turtles.

   (c) Some turtles are reptiles.

   (d) Some tortoises are turtles.

2. If an animal has slim, flat feet with webbed toes, there is a good chance that the animal

   (a) can run fast.

   (b) lives on land.

   (c) is a tortoise.

   (d) lives in water.

3. This story is mainly about

   (a) turtle shells.

   (b) primitive reptiles.

   (c) a special type of turtle.

   (d) what a tortoise eats and why.

4. What is a predator?

   (a) something primitive

   (b) something without a skeleton

   (c) something that is not a mammal

   (d) something that eats or kills other animals

5. Think about how the word **walking** relates to the word **plodding**. Which words relate in the same way?

walking : plodding

   (a) eating : chewing

   (b) swimming : flying

   (c) running : jogging

   (d) reading : looking

Hidden Treasure—Right Before Our Eyes!

New words to practice.
Say each word ten times.

* obvious
* ancient
* astronomer
* centuries

* constellation
* museum
* statue
* shoulders

Choose one new word to write.

_____

- -

_____

Hidden Treasure—Right Before Our Eyes!

"I can't see the forest because of the trees." Have you ever heard this saying? We say it when we miss something obvious. If something is obvious, it is easy. It is plain to see. It is easy to understand. Sometimes this saying can be said about science. An important star map was lost long ago. An ancient Greek astronomer made the map. His name was Hipparchus. He made the map 21 centuries ago. The map showed constellations on it. A constellation is a group of stars.

There is a museum in Naples, Italy. In the museum, there is a statue. The statue is very old. The statue is ancient, but it is a copy of an even older statue! It is a copy of an old Greek statue. There is an old Greek myth about Atlas. Atlas had to hold up the world forever. The statue shows Atlas holding the world on his shoulders.

An astronomer named Bradley went to the museum. He looked at the statue. He looked at the world Atlas was holding on his shoulders. He saw constellations on it. Suddenly, Bradley thought, "Could this be the lost map? Could the globe that everyone has been looking at be a hidden treasure?"

Bradley measured 70 points on the world Atlas carried. The points matched stars. Then, Bradley figured out how much the constellations had moved over the centuries. What did Bradley find? He found that the map matched a night sky of long ago. It matched what the night sky would have looked like above Greece around 125 B.C. This was the time Hipparchus was working!

We know that Hipparchus made small globes. He put his star maps on the globes. No one else at that time knew as much about the stars as Hipparchus. Bradley thinks that the artist copied one of the globes. The star map was lost for centuries, but it was right before our eyes! It was a hidden treasure for all to see. Do you think it is a case of not seeing the forest for the trees?

Hidden Treasure—Right Before Our Eyes!

After reading the story, answer the questions.
Fill in the circle next to the correct answer.

1. This story is mainly about

   (a) a lost map.

   (b) Hipparchus.

   (c) constellations.

   (d) an astronomer named Bradley.

2. How many points did Bradley measure on the world Atlas carried?

   (a) 21

   (b) 70

   (c) 100

   (d) 125

3. What sentence would Bradley most likely agree with?

   (a) Looking at art is not important.

   (b) Artists do not care about science.

   (c) Art and science are both important.

   (d) Astronomers should spend more time looking at stars.

4. Think about how the word **centuries** relates to **years**. Which words relate in the same way?

centuries : years

   (a) days : nights

   (b) world : globe

   (c) tree : forest

   (d) months : days

5. A globe is

   (a) ancient.

   (b) the world.

   (c) a star map.

   (d) anything shaped like a ball.

Where You Can Run Away from Night

New words to practice.
Say each word ten times.

* solar system   * axis

* orbits   * imagine

* avoid   * equator

* rotates   * acid

Choose one new word to write.

_____

- - - - - - - - - - - - - - - - - - -

_____

Where You Can Run Away from Night

Venus is a planet. It is in our solar system. It orbits around the sun. All the planets in our solar system orbit around the sun. Venus is the second planet from the Sun in our solar system. Earth is the third planet. Venus is close to Earth in size, but Venus is very different. On Venus, you can avoid nightfall. You can run away from the night.

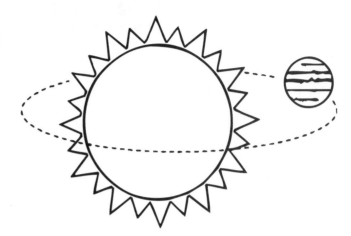

As a planet orbits around the sun, it rotates on its own axis. We call the time it takes the Earth to spin around a day. Our days are 24 hours long. Earth rotates on its axis every 24 hours. Venus has the slowest spin of any body in our solar system. It takes Venus 243 of our days to rotate just once. This means that one day on Venus is 243 of our days long!

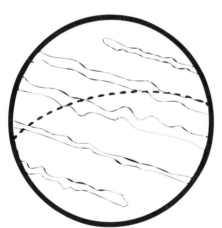

Imagine something. Imagine that you are on Venus's equator. The equator is an imaginary line. It goes around the middle of a planet. The line divides a planet into two. Venus's equator moves at just 4 miles (6.4 kilometers) per hour. This means that if you were a good, fast runner, you could run faster than Venus spins! You could avoid seeing nightfall. You could run away from the night!

A year is the time it takes a planet to travel around the sun. Our year is 365 days. A year on Venus is equal to 225 of our days. Remember that a day on Venus is equal to 243 of our Earth days. This means that on Venus a day is longer than a year! If you were from Venus, you would have your first birthday before you were one day old!

Probes have been sent to Venus. We know that Venus is the hottest planet. Acid rain falls from the clouds. The acid rain would burn us. We could not live there. After the sun and the moon, Venus is the brightest thing in the sky. Sometimes we can see it with the naked eye.

Where You Can Run Away from Night

After reading the story, answer the questions.
Fill in the circle next to the correct answer.

1. A year on Venus is equal to how many of our Earth days?

   (a) 24
   (b) 225
   (c) 243
   (d) 365

2. What is not true about Venus?

   (a) It is third from the sun.
   (b) It is the hottest planet.
   (c) A day is longer than a year.
   (d) It is the brightest thing in the sky after the sun and moon.

3. This story is mainly about

   (a) Venus.
   (b) running.
   (c) our solar system.
   (d) how long a day is.

4. The word *avoid* means

   (a) to look for.
   (b) to keep going.
   (c) to keep away from.
   (d) to rotate on an axis.

5. Think about how the word **hottest** relates to **coldest**. Which words relate in the same way?

hottest : coldest

   (a) sun : planet
   (b) water : wettest
   (c) fastest : slowest
   (d) brightest : Venus

Meat-Eating
Plants Vocabulary

New words to practice.
Say each word ten times.

* halves   * carnivorous

* carbon dioxide   * decaying

* minerals   * active

* another   * passive

Choose one new word to write.

_____

- -

_____

Meat-Eating Plants

A black fly smells something good. The smell is coming from a plant. It is a sweet smell. The black fly lands on one of the plant's leaves. The black fly wants to eat. Suddenly, the leaf moves! The two halves of the leaf clamp together. They trap the fly! The fly wanted to eat something sweet. Instead, the plant eats the fly.

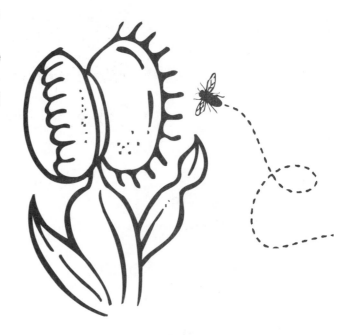

Plants get energy from sunlight. Plants use energy from sunlight to change water and carbon dioxide into food. Most plants get their water from soil. Carbon dioxide is a gas. Plants get their carbon dioxide from the air. The carbon dioxide goes into tiny openings in the plant's leaves. Plants also need minerals. Minerals are natural. They are nonliving. Most plants get their minerals from the soil.

What happens if a plant lives in an area where the soil does not have all the minerals it needs? The plant needs to get its minerals another way. Carnivorous plants get their minerals another way. Carnivorous plants eat meat. Carnivorous plants get their minerals from animals they trap and kill.

How does a carnivorous plant get insects or other animals to come to it? Some plants smell good. They smell like nectar. The nectar smell attracts flies, bees, and ants. Other plants smell bad. They smell like something decaying. When something is decaying, it is rotting. Many insects and animals like the smell of decay. Some carnivorous plants have active traps. Active traps move. Two halves of a leaf may clamp together. One leaf may swing shut like a trapdoor.

Other carnivorous plants have passive traps. Passive traps do not have moving parts. A passive trap may be sticky. The animal gets stuck and cannot move. Some passive traps have leaves shaped a special way. The leaves make a one-way tunnel. The animals go into the tunnel because they are attracted to the smell. Then, they are trapped. They cannot turn around and get out. They become food for the plant.

Meat-Eating Plants

**After reading the story, answer the questions.
Fill in the circle next to the correct answer.**

1. This story is mainly about

   (a) minerals.

   (b) carnivorous plants.

   (c) active and passive traps.

   (d) how plants get their energy.

2. A plant has a sticky leaf. An insect gets stuck on the leaf. This would be an example of

   (a) a passive trap.

   (b) an active trap.

   (c) leaves shaped a special way.

   (d) two leaf halves clamping together.

3. What is it that carnivorous plants need from insects or animals?

   (a) water

   (b) energy

   (c) minerals

   (d) carbon dioxide

4. What thing would most likely smell like it was decaying?

   (a) hot rice

   (b) an old chair

   (c) a rotten apple

   (d) a yellow banana

5. Think about how the word **active** relates to **passive**. Which words relate in the same way?

active : passive

   (a) move : run

   (b) busy : still

   (c) sick : doctor

   (d) energy : sunlight

Harnessing the Wind

New words to practice.

Say each word ten times.

✳ mechanical	✳ invented
✳ device	✳ countries
✳ harness	✳ square
✳ windmill	✳ triangle

Choose one new word to write.

_____

- - - - - - - - - - - - - - - - - - - -

_____

Harnessing the Wind

A mechanical device was built long ago. A device is something made or invented for a special use. Tools are devices. Machines are devices. The mechanical device was the first one to use wind as its source of power. It harnessed the wind. It controlled the wind. It used the wind for energy. What was the mechanical device?

Most people think the answer is a windmill. A windmill is a mechanical device. It harnesses the wind. It was the first machine to use wind power to do work on land. It was invented long ago. It was invented in about the seventh century. It was invented in the countries we know today as Iran and Afghanistan. The early windmills were used to grind grain between heavy stones. They were used to pump water from rivers, too. Windmills are still used in many countries today.

The windmill was the first machine to use wind power on land. It was not the first mechanical device to use wind power. The first mechanical device to harness the wind's energy was probably the sailboat. The first sails were simple squares. You could only sail in the direction of the wind with the simple square sails.

Arab sailors invented new sails. The sails were not squares. They were shaped more like triangles. Triangles have three sides. With the triangular sail, a sailor could go in any direction. Sailors could go far with their new sails. They could trade with people in far away countries.

Where does the wind come from? As the earth spins, the sun warms it. The earth is heated unevenly. Why? Places not covered with clouds heat up faster. Also, land warms up faster than the sea. This is because water is always moving. The moving water carries the heat away. The hot surface of the earth heats up the air above it. Hot air rises. When the hot air rises, cold air rushes in to take its place. Winds are moving air.

Harnessing the Wind

After reading the story, answer the questions.
Fill in the circle next to the correct answer.

1. This story is mainly about
   - (a) windmills.
   - (b) two kinds of sails.
   - (c) where winds come from.
   - (d) two devices used to harness the wind.

2. About what century was the windmill invented?
   - (a) first
   - (b) third
   - (c) fifth
   - (d) seventh

3. Think about how the word **triangle** relates to **three**. Which words relate in the same way?

   > **triangle : three**

   - (a) square : four
   - (b) windmill : sails
   - (c) harness : control
   - (d) machine : mechanical device

4. What is one reason the earth is heated unevenly?
   - (a) The earth spins unevenly.
   - (b) Cold air rises faster than hot air.
   - (c) Water does not heat up as fast as land.
   - (d) Clouds keep the hot air at the surface.

5. What would be an example of a mechanical device?
   - (a) a bike
   - (b) a tree
   - (c) the wind
   - (d) a pair of shoes

A Dinner of Mice

New words to practice.

Say each word ten times.

* arctic	* stomach
* wilderness	* healthy
* caribou	* crave
* regurgitated	* dissected

Choose one new word to write.

_____

- -

_____

A Dinner of Mice

The pilot let Farley out of the tiny plane. Snow and ice were all around. There were no people. The pilot said he would come back for Farley in the fall sometime. Before the plane took off, Farley asked the pilot where they were. The pilot said, "Sorry about that. Don't quite know myself. No maps of this country anyway."

Farley Mowat had come to study wolves. He was in Canada.   He was in the arctic wilderness. Farley wanted to observe wolves in the arctic wilderness. How did they survive? What did they eat? Did they feast on caribou? Caribou are large deer. They are related to reindeer.

Over time, Farley learned where the wolves lived. Sometimes he got very close to them. He saw them eating mice. Farley was surprised to see them eating mice. Ootek, a man who lived in the Arctic, told Farley that wolves eat many mice. He told Farley that the wolves carry the mice home to their pups in their bellies. They fed their pups regurgitated mice. When something is regurgitated, it is thrown up. Partly digested food is brought from the stomach back up the mouth.

Was a mouse diet healthy? As an experiment, Farley began to eat only mice! After one week of only mice, Farley began to crave fats. Farley remembered that the wolves ate the entire mouse. Farley was eating only the meaty parts. Farley had dissected mice. He had cut them open. When Farley dissected the mice he saw where the mice stored their fat. It was stored in the stomach area. Farley began to eat the entire mouse except for the skin. Farley stopped wanting fats. He did not crave them anymore.

Farley learned many things about the wolves. He learned that they ate caribou, but they ate other things, too. They ate mice and ground squirrels. They even ate fish! When wolves ate caribou, they usually ate the weak and sick ones. These caribou were the easiest to hunt. By eating the weak caribou, the wolves helped the caribou herds stay healthy.

A Dinner of Mice

**After reading the story, answer the questions.
Fill in the circle next to the correct answer.**

1. This story is mainly about

  ⓐ eating mice.

  ⓑ a country without maps.

  ⓒ what wolves eat in the arctic.

  ⓓ how caribou herds stay healthy.

2. When you crave something, you want it badly. What did Farley crave after eating mice for one week?

  ⓐ fat

  ⓑ meat

  ⓒ skin

  ⓓ caribou

3. Think about how the word **wolf** relates to **den**. Which words relate in the same way?

  > **wolf : den**

  ⓐ fish : hunt

  ⓑ bird : nest

  ⓒ stomach : fat

  ⓓ caribou : herd

4. What is the best answer for why Farley wanted the pilot to leave him in the wilderness?

  ⓐ He wanted to be in a country without maps.

  ⓑ He wanted to see if a mouse diet was healthy.

  ⓒ He wanted to see wolves regurgitate food to their pups.

  ⓓ He wanted to observe wolves over time in the wilderness.

5. What answer is in the right story order?

  ⓐ Farley saw wolves; the pilot dropped Farley off; Farley ate mice.

  ⓑ Farley saw caribou; Farley met Ooteck; Farley got close to wolves.

  ⓒ Farley got close to wolves; Farley saw wolves eat mice; Farley craved fats.

  ⓓ The pilot dropped Farley off; Farley saw wolves regurgitate mice; Ooteck dissected mice.

How to See Through a Wall

New words to practice.

Say each word ten times.

＊ through	＊ certain
＊ impossible	＊ materials
＊ substance	＊ obsidian
＊ fusing	＊ archeologists

Choose one new word to write.

_____

- - - - - - - - - - - - - - - - - -

_____

How to See Through a Wall

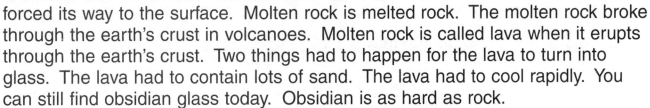

"I can see through a wall," said Bea. Bea's friends laughed. They said it was impossible to see through a wall. Bea said, "It is not impossible. It is possible. It is easy. You can see through a wall, too. You can see through a wall because there is sand."

It is not possible to see through all walls. It is impossible to see through a wall without windows. Windows make it possible! Windows are made of glass. What is glass made of? Glass is made mostly of sand! Glass is a substance made by fusing certain materials together. When something is fused it is melted together. To make glass, sand and other materials are fused together. They are heated up and mixed. After fusing, the mixture is cooled. The result is glass.

The first glass was made in nature. It is a volcanic substance. It is called obsidian. Obsidian was formed when molten rock in the core of the earth forced its way to the surface. Molten rock is melted rock. The molten rock broke through the earth's crust in volcanoes. Molten rock is called lava when it erupts through the earth's crust. Two things had to happen for the lava to turn into glass. The lava had to contain lots of sand. The lava had to cool rapidly. You can still find obsidian glass today. Obsidian is as hard as rock.

People long ago learned how to make glass. Archeologists study how people lived long ago. Archeologists have found glass in Egypt that was made over 4,000 years ago! Just like today, the Egyptians heated certain materials. They fused them together. Then they cooled the mixture.

Glass is shaped when it is poured into molds. It can be pressed, rolled, and blown, too. Long ago, window glass was hand blown. The blower blew a long tube of glass. The tube was split and flattened. How big were these sheets of glass? It depended on the lungpower of the glass blower!

How to See Through a Wall

After reading the story, answer the questions.
Fill in the circle next to the correct answer.

1. Where would you most likely find obsidian?

   (a) where there are walls
   (b) where Egyptians lived
   (c) where volcanoes erupted
   (d) where glass blowers worked

2. When something is fused,

   (a) it is melted together.
   (b) it is found by archeologists.
   (c) it erupts from the earth's surface.
   (d) it is shaped and poured into molds.

3. This story is mainly about

   (a) glass.
   (b) obsidian.
   (c) how to see through walls.
   (d) fusing certain materials.

4. Different colors of glass are probably made by

   (a) heating and cooling.
   (b) certain materials in the mixture.
   (c) the way the glass is molded or shaped.
   (d) rock breaking through the earth's crust.

5. Think about how the word **hot** relates to **cold**. Which words relate in the same way?

hot : cold

   (a) fuse : melt
   (b) window : wall
   (c) archeologis t: glass
   (d) impossible : possible

Night Animals

New words to practice.
Say each word ten times.

* nocturnal   * twice

* active   * mirror

* diurnal   * tapetum

* sensitive   * bounces

Choose one new word to write.

_____

- -

_____

Night Animals

Night animals spend most of their lives in the dark. They sleep during the day. Then, when it is night, they wake up. They hunt and eat. They build their nests. They take care of their babies, all in the dark. Night animals are nocturnal. They are active at night. Night animals are not diurnal. They are not active during the day.

Who has a better sense of sight—a nocturnal or a diurnal animal? A nocturnal animal has a better sense of sight. All eyes have a lens. The lens gathers light. All eyes have many tiny cells at their back. The tiny cells are called rods. The rods are sensitive to light. Nocturnal animals have a lot more rods than diurnal animals. With more rods, nocturnal animals are more sensitive to light. They can see with little light.

Some nocturnal animals can see every ray of light twice! This makes it so they can see when there is less light. How can an animal see every ray of light twice? The animal has a kind of mirror. The mirror is in the back of its eye. The mirror is called a tapetum. First, the light enters the eye. It hits the rods. Then, it bounces off the mirror. It bounces off the mirror and hits the rods again. Have you ever wondered why some nocturnal animal eyes seem to glow at night when you shine a light at them? Now you know! It is because the light is bouncing off of the tapetum!

Many nocturnal animals have big ears. This makes it so they can hear sounds from far away. Cats are nocturnal hunters. They need to be quiet so their big-eared prey cannot hear them. The bottoms of cats' paws have heavy fur and soft pads. The fur and the pads help the cats move quietly.

Nocturnal animals have a good sense of smell and touch. The catfish is a nocturnal hunter. Its "whiskers" are not hair. They are flesh. The catfish uses them to feel and smell its way along the river bottom.

Night Animals

After reading the story, answer the questions.
Fill in the circle next to the correct answer.

1. What sense was not in the story?

   ⓐ tasting

   ⓑ hearing

   ⓒ smelling

   ⓓ touching

2. This story is mainly about

   ⓐ light sensitive cells.

   ⓑ when animals are active.

   ⓒ nocturnal animal senses.

   ⓓ how animals hunt at night.

3. Why do some animal's eyes glow when you shine a light at them?

   ⓐ The animal has more rods in its eyes.

   ⓑ The animal's eyes are sensitive to light.

   ⓒ The ray of light bounces off of the tapetum.

   ⓓ The ray of light hits tiny cells in the eye lens.

4. Think about how the word **nocturnal** relates to **night**. Which words relate in the same way?

nocturnal : night

   ⓐ eye : sense

   ⓑ pad : quiet

   ⓒ twice : two

   ⓓ diurnal : day

5. Many hawks and eagles fly high in the sky while looking for animals to eat, or prey. This means they are most likely

   ⓐ mirrors.

   ⓑ diurnal.

   ⓒ nocturnal.

   ⓓ sensitive.

What the Letters Mean

New words to practice.

Say each word ten times.

* elements   * symbol

* atoms   * calcium

* chart   * oxygen

* Periodic Table   * placeholder

Choose one new word to write.

_____

- -

_____

What the Letters Mean

Long ago people thought that earth, wind, fire, and water were basic elements. They thought earth, wind, fire, and water made up all matter. Matter is anything that takes up space and has weight. Today we know this is not true. All matter is made up of elements. The elements are not earth, wind, fire, and water.

Elements are made up of atoms. Atoms are very small. Each element is made up of one type of atom. There are over 100 elements. All the elements are on a chart. The chart has a name. The chart is called the Periodic Table of the Elements. Every element on the Periodic Table has a name. The elements have a number, too.

Each element has a symbol. The symbol is one or two letters. For some, the symbol is the first letter or letters of the element's name. Calcium is Ca. Calcium helps make our bones strong. Aluminum is Al. A lot of cans are made out of aluminum. Oxygen is O. We breathe oxygen. It is in our air.

Some of the symbols may seem very odd. They are odd, but they all have a story. Ag is silver. In Latin, the word for silver is *argentum*. Helium's symbol is He. Helium is named after Helios. Helios was the Greek god of the sun. Both Einstein and Curie were famous scientists. Do you see their names in Einsteinium and Curium? These elements are known as Es and Cu.

What happens when a new element is found? It is given a placeholder name. The placeholder names may seem odd. The names come from Latin. The name is the same as the element number. For example, element number 111 is called unununium. In Latin, this means *one one one*. The symbol is Uuu. Element 112 is called ununbium. This means *one one two*. The symbol is Uub. When people are sure the new element is real, the person who found it gets to think of a name. A group of scientists then decide if the name is okay.

H																	He
Li	Be											B	C	N	O	F	Ne
Na	Mg											Al	Si	P	S	Cl	Ar
K	Ca	Se	Ti	V	Cr	Mn	Fe	Co	Ni	Cu	Zn	Ga	Ge	As	Se	Br	Kr
Rb	Sr	Y	Zr	Nb	Mo	Tc	Ru	Rh	Pd	Ag	Cd	In	Sn	Sb	Te	I	Xe
Cs	Ba		Hf	Ta	W	Re	Os	Ir	Pt	Au	Hg	Tl	Pb	Bi	Po	At	Rn
Fr	Ra		Rf	Db	Sg	Bh	Hs	Mt	Uun	Uuu	Uub						

La	Ce	Pr	Nd	Prr	Sm	Eu	Gd	Tb	Dy	Ho	Er	Tm	Yb	Lu
Ac	Th	Pa	U	Np	Pu	Arr	Cm	Bk	Cf	Es	Fm	Md	No	Lr

What the Letters Mean

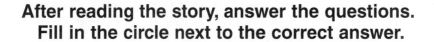

After reading the story, answer the questions.
Fill in the circle next to the correct answer.

1. The Periodic Table of the Elements

   ⓐ has over 200 elements.

   ⓑ has no place for new elements.

   ⓒ has the elements earth and fire.

   ⓓ has the symbol and number of all the known elements.

2. This story is mainly about

   ⓐ element names

   ⓑ placeholder names

   ⓒ elements and their symbols

   ⓓ earth, wind, fire, and water

3. Placeholder names

   ⓐ are made from Greek number words.

   ⓑ are made by the person who finds the new element.

   ⓒ hold the number place of the element until a name is found.

   ⓓ become the name of the element when people are sure the element is real.

4. What is not true of elements?

   ⓐ Elements make up all matter.

   ⓑ All elements are made of atoms.

   ⓒ Elements have symbols and numbers.

   ⓓ Scientists have found all the elements.

5. Think about how the word **element** relates to **symbol**. Which words relate in the same way?

element : symbol

   ⓐ cat : tail

   ⓑ child : name

   ⓒ house : door

   ⓓ atom : small

The Midnight Sun

New words to practice.
Say each word ten times.

* summer   * tilts

* winter   * toward

* orbits   * northern

* axis   * hemisphere

Choose one new word to write.

_____

- -

_____

The Midnight Sun

Victor lives in the far north of Norway. In the summer, Victor does not go to bed when it gets dark. Victor can't because it does not get dark! In the winter, Victor does not get up when the sun comes up. Victor can't because the sun never rises! Why are Victor's summers and winters like this?

Our Earth orbits the sun. As it orbits the sun, our Earth spins on its axis. Earth's axis is an imaginary straight line that passes through the North and South poles. As the Earth spins, half of it faces the sun. It is in daylight. The other half is away from the sun. It is in darkness. The Earth makes a complete circle in a day or 24 hours.

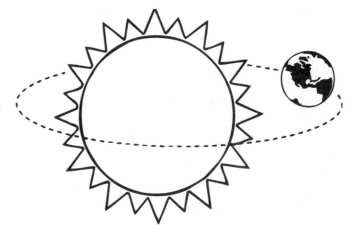

Norway is close to the North Pole. Daylight hours and seasons depend on how the Earth tilts toward the sun. The North Pole tilts toward the sun for six months. This means that light from the sun does not have to travel as far to the north side of the Earth. The days in the Northern Hemisphere are longer. They are warmer, too. In the far north, the tilt of the Earth's axis is such that the sun never sets. This is called the midnight sun.

The South Pole tilts toward the sun for six months, too. When the South Pole is tilting toward the sun, it is summer in the Southern Hemisphere. In the Northern Hemisphere, where Victor lives, it is winter. The days are colder and shorter. During December and January the sun never rises over the horizon.

Many places use a clock with the numbers 1 through 24. Each number is one hour of the day. The letters A.M. and P.M. are not used. The first hours of the day are numbers 1 through 12. The last hours of the day are 12 through 24. 2:00 P.M., for example, would be 14:00. Midnight, or 12:00 A.M., would be 24:00. Sometimes Victor cannot tell night from day by looking at the sun. A clock with 24 numbers makes sense.

The Midnight Sun

After reading the story, answer the questions.
Fill in the circle next to the correct answer.

1. What is not true of Earth's axis?

   (a) It is imaginary.

   (b) It is not straight.

   (c) The Earth spins on its axis.

   (d) It passes through the North and South poles.

2. What time would you most likely be in school?

   (a) 5:00 or 5:00 A.M.

   (b) 17:00 or 5:00 P.M.

   (c) 10:00 or 10:00 A.M.

   (d) 22:00 or 10:00 P.M.

3. This story is mainly about

   (a) Victor.

   (b) how the Earth spins on its axis.

   (c) clocks with numbers 1 through 24.

   (d) Why Victor's summers and winters are the way they are.

4. If it is winter in the Northern Hemisphere

   (a) the South Pole is tilting toward the sun.

   (b) the North Pole is tilting toward the sun.

   (c) the Earth is spinning more slowly in the Southern Hemisphere.

   (d) the sun is not setting below the horizon in the Northern Hemisphere.

5. Think about how the word **summer** relates to **cold**. Which words relate in the same way?

summer : cold

   (a) tilt : axis

   (b) winter : hot

   (c) clock : time

   (d) sun : midnight

Passing Gas

New words to practice.

Say each word ten times.

* operation
* healthy
* intestines
* bacteria

* produced
* volume
* release
* milliliters

Choose one new word to write.

_____

- - - - - - - - - - - - - - - - - -

_____

Passing Gas

You have just had an operation. The doctor asks, "How are you? Are you getting better after the operation? Are you healthy? Have you passed gas yet?" Did you hear the doctor right? Did the doctor really ask if you had passed gas? Yes, you did hear the doctor. The doctor did ask if you had passed gas. The doctor knows something. He or she knows that if you can pass gas, your intestines have started working. It is a sign that you are healing from your operation.

We have lots of bacteria in our bodies. The bacteria are tiny. We cannot see them. Some bacteria can harm us, but other bacteria can help us. Good bacteria in our large intestines help us break down food. Sometimes when the food is broken down, a gas is produced.

A gas is not a solid. A gas is not a liquid. A gas is a state of matter that has no definite shape or volume. Some foods produce more gas than other foods when they are broken down. Even healthy foods can produce a lot of gas. When the amount of gas builds up, your body wants to get rid of it. It wants the gas to pass out of your body.

Volume is the amount of space an object takes up. Volume is often measured in liters or milliliters. How much gas does a person release at one time? A healthy person releases almost half a cup. This is about .12 liters or 120 milliliters. In one day, healthy people produce about 2 cups of gas. This is close to half a liter or 500 milliliters.

People are not the only animals that pass gas. All animals pass gas. The amount of gas other animals produce depends on what they eat. The types of food animals eat can change the way the gas smells. The types of food animals eat can change how much gas is produced, too.

Passing Gas

After reading the story, answer the questions.
Fill in the circle next to the correct answer.

1. Why would a doctor ask if you had passed gas?

  ⓐ to see if you needed an operation

  ⓑ to see if your intestines are working properly

  ⓒ to see if you are eating healthy food

  ⓓ to see if you had bad bacteria in your body

2. This story is mainly about

  ⓐ passing gas.

  ⓑ being healthy.

  ⓒ what a gas is.

  ⓓ bacteria in our body.

3. Other animals pass gas so it is probably true that

  ⓐ some animals do not have intestines.

  ⓑ sometimes other animals do not eat healthy foods.

  ⓒ other animals produce the same amount of gas we do.

  ⓓ other animals have a bacteria good for them in their intestines.

4. If you were told something had no definite shape or volume, it is a

  ⓐ gas

  ⓑ solid

  ⓒ liquid

  ⓓ bacteria

5. Think about how the word **produce** relates to **make**. Which words relate in the same way?

produce : make

  ⓐ cook : eat

  ⓑ gas : solid

  ⓒ release : let go

  ⓓ pass : break down

The Walrus

New words to practice.

Say each word ten times.

* preserver   * marine

* walrus   * ivory

* pouches   * valuable

* pinniped   * naturally

Choose one new word to write.

_____

- -

_____

The Walrus

How are a life preserver and a walrus alike? Many life preservers are filled with air. They fit around your neck, and they help you float. A walrus has built in "life preservers"! A walrus has air pouches around its neck. The walrus can fill the pouches with air. The air and the walrus's blubber, or fat, is enough to keep the huge beast afloat. The walrus fills its air pouches and floats when it is feeling ill or when it wants to sleep at sea.

A walrus is a pinniped. Seals and sea lions are pinnipeds, too. Pinnipeds do not have arms or legs. They have flippers. The flippers look like fins, and that is how pinnipeds got their names. The word *pinniped* means "fin-footed." All pinnipeds live in two different worlds. They are marine mammals. They live both in the water and on land.

All walruses live in the far north. It gets very cold in the far north, but the walrus does not mind. The walrus's blubber helps it stay warm. Even in high winds and in 31 degree below zero (–35 degrees Celsius) weather, walruses have been seen sleeping happily on the ice.

Walruses are the only pinnipeds that have tusks. The tusks are ivory and very valuable. Walruses were hunted for their tusks. The ivory tusks are just two teeth in the upper jaw that don't stop growing. Big walruses have tusks three feet (one meter) long! They weigh over 13 pounds (5.9 kilograms). Walruses use their tusks when they fight. Their tusks are also valuable when it comes to finding food. They use their tusks to stir up mud on the ocean floor. Then, they eat any shellfish they find.

A pinniped is a marine mammal, so it spends a lot of time in the water. A pinniped can open and close its nose. On land, they open their nose. In water, they close it. You live on land so your nose is naturally open. A pinniped's nose is naturally closed. It uses special muscles to open it when it is on land.

88

The Walrus

**After reading the story, answer the questions.
Fill in the circle next to the correct answer.**

1. This story is mainly about

   (a) pinnipeds.

   (b) the walrus.

   (c) how a walrus is a marine mammal.

   (d) how a walrus and life preserver are alike.

2. What animal is *not* a pinniped?

   (a) a seal

   (b) a fish

   (c) a walrus

   (d) a sea lion

3. Think about how the word **float** relates to **sink**. Which words relate in the same way?

   > **float : sink**

   (a) fix : break

   (b) ivory : tusk

   (c) arm : flipper

   (d) cold : blubber

4. The walrus is a marine mammal. What does the word *marine* mean?

   (a) of or found on land

   (b) of or found on the ice

   (c) of or found in the water

   (d) of or found in the far north

5. When might you find a walrus floating?

   (a) when it is looking for food

   (b) when its air pouches are empty

   (c) when it is looking for shellfish

   (d) when it is feeling ill or sleeping

Clothes Stronger than Steel

New words to practice.

Say each word ten times.

* Kevlar   * substances

* natural   * refine

* materials   * extract

* mixture   * chemicals

Choose one new word to write.

_____

- -

_____

Clothes Stronger than Steel

A man is wearing a vest. The vest is very strong. It is made out of Kevlar. Kevlar is very lightweight. It is not heavy. It is five times stronger than steel. It is strong enough to stop bullets. Kevlar is also used in spacecraft construction. Spacecrafts need to be light and strong. Kevlar is a good material for spacecrafts because it is light and strong.

What is Kevlar? We get wool for our clothes from sheep. Does Kevlar come from an animal? We get cotton and linen for our clothes from plants. Does Kevlar come from plants? We get silk from silkworms for our clothes. Does Kevlar come from a worm? Can we find Kevlar in a forest? Can we pick it up from the ground like a rock?

You cannot find Kevlar in nature. Kevlar is not natural. It is manmade. When something is manmade it is a mix of different materials. Scientists take different natural materials and mix them together in new ways. Sometimes they heat the mixture. Heat often makes it possible for different materials to combine into new ones. Sometimes they cool the mixture. They experiment. They make new substances. Often, the new substances do not behave like the old materials. The new substances behave in a new way.

Kevlar is a type of plastic. Kevlar is related to nylon. Nylon is a type of plastic, too. Lots of our clothes today are made with nylon. We make plastic from oil we get from the ground. Oil from the ground is crude oil. It is black and sticky. We refine the oil. When we refine the oil, we process it. We clean it. We refine it so we can use it.

When we refine oil, we sort the oil into parts. The parts have different boiling points. Some parts boil at different temperatures than others. We also extract different chemicals from the oil. When something is extracted, it is taken out. We use the chemicals we extract to make plastic and other new substances.

Clothes Stronger than Steel

After reading the story, answer the questions.
Fill in the circle next to the correct answer.

1. This story is mainly about

   ⓐ oil.

   ⓑ a vest.

   ⓒ new substances.

   ⓓ natural materials.

2. From the story you can tell that clothes worn long ago

   ⓐ were warmer than they are today.

   ⓑ were made from natural materials.

   ⓒ were lighter than they are today.

   ⓓ were stronger than they are today.

3. Think about how the word **extract** relates to **out**. What words relate in the same way?

   | **extract : out** |

   ⓐ add : in

   ⓑ see : look

   ⓒ heat : boil

   ⓓ jump : leap

4. What is nylon made from?

   ⓐ Kevlar

   ⓑ plastic

   ⓒ crude oil

   ⓓ spacecrafts

5. If you combine two materials and make a new substance, the new substance

   ⓐ will be refined.

   ⓑ will behave the same.

   ⓒ will have the same boiling point.

   ⓓ will sometimes behave in a new way.

Tsunami

New words to practice.

Say each word ten times.

* energy

* particles

* tumble

* circle

* tsunami

* column

* shallow

* earthquake

Choose one new word to write.

_____

- -

_____

Tsunami

Do you think of energy when you look at a wave? A wave is one way that energy moves from place to place. It looks like a wave pushes water to the shore. A wave does not push water forward. Think about a gull sitting on the water. The gull bobs up and down. It does not move forward. The gull and the water stay in the same place.

A wave is made up of tiny bits of water. The tiny bits are water particles. The energy of the wave makes the particles tumble in a circle. The particles tumble around in circles as the wave passes through. Most waves are made when the wind blows across the water. These waves are close to the water's surface. They are wind-driven.

Tsunamis are a different type of wave. They are not wind-driven. Tsunamis start when a force pushes energy through a column of water. The energy moves up. The energy flows outward. It flows outward from the center in large circles. Waves spread in all directions. The waves may stretch down to the ocean floor. They may stretch for thousands of miles or kilometers across the ocean.

In the open ocean, a tsunami's waves may be only three feet (one meter) high. They may be nothing more than small humps rolling across the water. The waves change near land. The ocean becomes shallow. The bottom of the waves begins to drag on the shallow floor. This slows down the lower part of the waves. The tops of the waves keep going. They grow taller. They can become killer waves. They can toss rocks onto shore. They can toss boats onto shore. They can crush houses.

Earthquakes are the most common cause of a tsunami. On December 26, 2004, a big earthquake struck. It was on the floor of the Indian Ocean. The movement disturbed a huge column of water. Huge waves spread out. They hit the shores of close and far away countries. More than 310,000 people were killed. It was the deadliest tsunami in recorded history.

Tsunami

**After reading the story, answer the questions.
Fill in the circle next to the correct answer.**

1. What causes a wave to change when it nears land?

   ⓐ The wave starts getting taller.

   ⓑ The energy making the wave is used up.

   ⓒ The water particles start tumbling faster.

   ⓓ The bottom part of the wave begins to drag on the shallow floor.

2. A tsunami is

   ⓐ a wind-driven wave.

   ⓑ a form of energy moving from place to place.

   ⓒ nothing more than small humps rolling across the water.

   ⓓ water particles tumbling only in circles close to the surface.

3. This story is mainly about

   ⓐ energy.

   ⓑ earthquakes.

   ⓒ how water particles move.

   ⓓ different types of waves.

4. What happened December 26, 2004?

   ⓐ More than 310,000 people were killed.

   ⓑ A huge column of water was disturbed.

   ⓒ A tsunami started an earthquake on the ocean floor.

   ⓓ An earthquake struck the surface of the Indian Ocean.

5. Think about how the word **wave** relates to **tsunami**. Which words relate in the same way?

   wave : tsunami

   ⓐ bird : gull

   ⓑ energy : water

   ⓒ shallow : tall

   ⓓ earthquake : Indian

Flying Predators

New words to practice.

Say each word ten times.

✳ eagle	✳ predator
✳ talon	✳ prey
✳ feathers	✳ slippery
✳ ontinent	✳ wriggling

Choose one new word to write.

_____

- - - - - - - - - - - - - - - - - - -

_____

Flying Predators

What type of an eagle has rough bumps on its toes? What type of an eagle has short strong toes? What type of an eagle has huge claws or talons that are five inches (13 centimeters) long? What type of an eagle has feathers on its legs?

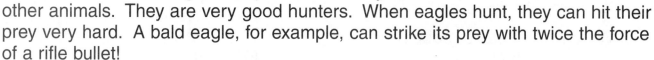

Eagles are found on every continent except one. Eagles do not live on the continent of Antarctica. They are found in deserts, jungles, swamps, and forests. Some eagles live in mountains, and some eagles live near the ocean. All eagles are predators. They eat other animals. They are very good hunters. When eagles hunt, they can hit their prey very hard. A bald eagle, for example, can strike its prey with twice the force of a rifle bullet!

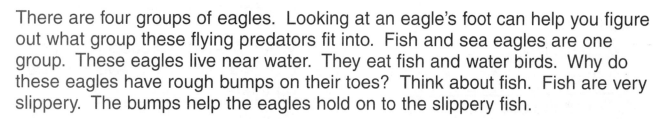

There are four groups of eagles. Looking at an eagle's foot can help you figure out what group these flying predators fit into. Fish and sea eagles are one group. These eagles live near water. They eat fish and water birds. Why do these eagles have rough bumps on their toes? Think about fish. Fish are very slippery. The bumps help the eagles hold on to the slippery fish.

Snake eagles hunt snakes most of the time. They also hunt lizards and frogs. Snake eagles live where they can find snakes to eat. Snake eagles usually swallow snakes whole. A wriggling snake is hard to hold. Snake eagle's short strong toes are perfect for keeping a tight hold on a wriggling snake. Harpy eagles are very big. They live in forests and prey on large mammals. They need big talons to grab onto monkeys and tree sloths. Sometimes they use their big talons to hunt deer!

Booted eagles make up the last group. This is the only group of eagles that has feathers on its legs. The feathers go down to the birds' feet like boots. Booted eagles are found almost everywhere eagles can live. Smaller booted eagles have smaller toes and claws for catching smaller prey. Bigger booted eagles have larger feet and talons for catching bigger prey.

Flying Predators

**After reading the story, answer the questions.
Fill in the circle next to the correct answer.**

1. This story is mainly about

   (a) predators.

   (b) catching prey.

   (c) where eagles live.

   (d) eagle groups and their feet.

2. What kind of eagle group sometimes hunts deer?

   (a) Harpy

   (b) Snake

   (c) Booted

   (d) Fish and sea

3. If an eagle has short strong toes, it probably

   (a) eats fish.

   (b) eats snakes.

   (c) eats small mammals.

   (d) eats large mammals.

4. Think about how the word **claw** relates to **talon**. Which words relate in the same way?

claw : talon

   (a) prey : eat

   (b) fish : water

   (c) tooth : tusk

   (d) snake : slippery

5. What might be a reason why fish or sea eagles don't have feathers on their legs?

   (a) The feathers would make the eagle too heavy.

   (b) The feathers would make it easier for a fish to see the eagle.

   (c) It would be easy for the feathers to get wet when the eagle hunted.

   (d) The feathers would make it hard for the eagle to hold a fish with its toes.

The Gas Giant

New words to practice.

Say each word ten times.

* Jupiter
* solar system
* gravity
* attraction

* object
* asteroid
* astronomers
* telescope

Choose one new word to write.

_____

- -

_____

The Gas Giant

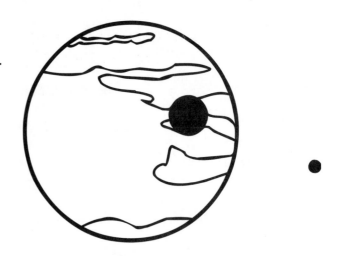

Over 1,000 planets the size of Earth could fit into it. What planet is it? Jupiter is the biggest planet in our solar system. All the planets in our solar system orbit around the Sun. Earth is third from the Sun. Jupiter is fifth from the Sun.

Jupiter is made mostly of gas. It is a gas giant. Gravity is a force of attraction. It is a force of attraction that pulls a smaller object toward a bigger one. Jupiter is so big that it is like a giant vacuum cleaner. Its gravitational force pulls on things around it. Asteroids are small, rocky objects. They orbit the sun. Any asteroid that comes near Jupiter is sucked into its atmosphere.

One moon orbits our planet Earth. It is held in its orbit by Earth's gravity. Jupiter has many moons. The moons are held in orbit by Jupiter's gravity. Astronomers have seen 16 moons. There may be more moons. Some of the moons are big. Some of the moons are little. One of Jupiter's moons is bigger than a planet. It is bigger than the planet Mercury! It is the biggest moon in the solar system.

We can see Jupiter without a telescope. We can see it with the naked eye. It looks like a bright star. Only the Sun, Moon, and Venus are brighter. A telescope helps us see things far away. You can see some of Jupiter's moons with a telescope. You can see a Great Red Spot, too. The spot is a big storm. It moves around. It swallows up other storms. It is getting smaller. It is only half as big as it was 100 years ago.

Astronomers have sent probes to Jupiter. The probes took pictures. The pictures were sent back to Earth. One mini-probe was sent down into Jupiter's atmosphere. The probe measured wind speed. It found out that winds on Jupiter are strong. They are stronger than any winds on Earth. They are strongest in the Great Red Spot. In the Great Red Spot, winds blow about 310 miles (500 kilometers) per hour!

The Gas Giant

After reading the story, answer the questions.
Fill in the circle next to the correct answer.

1. This story is mainly about
   - ⓐ a giant gas planet.
   - ⓑ Jupiter's Great Red Spot.
   - ⓒ what telescopes and probes have shown us.
   - ⓓ how many Earth sized planets could fit into Jupiter.

2. What planet is one of Jupiter's moons bigger than?
   - ⓐ Saturn
   - ⓑ Uranus
   - ⓒ Neptune
   - ⓓ Mercury

3. Think about how the word **planet** relates to **moon**. Which words relate in the same way?

planet : moon

   - ⓐ sun : planet
   - ⓑ star : probe
   - ⓒ orbit : atmosphere
   - ⓓ Jupiter : Great Red Spot

4. What object would have the greatest gravitational pull?
   - ⓐ Earth
   - ⓑ the Sun
   - ⓒ an asteroid
   - ⓓ Jupiter's largest moon

5. Why would someone probe something?
   - ⓐ to measure wind
   - ⓑ to take pictures
   - ⓒ to find out more about it
   - ⓓ to go down into the atmosphere

Who Mosquitoes Like to Bite

New words to practice.

Say each word ten times.

* investigate   * atoms

* experiment   * particles

* data   * molecules

* mosquitoes   * compounds

Choose one new word to write.

_____

- -

_____

Who Mosquitoes Like to Bite

Scientists learn things by asking questions. They investigate. They experiment. They collect data. Data is information. They look at the data. They use the data to help answer questions. Why do mosquitoes like some people better than others? Some scientists wanted to know. They wanted to investigate. They developed an experiment. They collected data. They used the data to help answer the question.

Matter is anything that takes up space and has weight. Atoms are small particles. We cannot see them. Atoms are the smallest particles to make up matter. Atoms can join with other atoms to make molecules. There are many different types of molecules. All molecules do not smell the same. Some smell more than others. Mosquitoes like certain molecules. They like certain molecules that come from our breath. They like certain molecules that come from our skin. They are attracted to their smell. They like the smell. They use the smell to find their victims.

Scientists put mosquitoes in tubes. The tubes were shaped like a Y. The mosquitoes were put at the base of the tube. The scientists put different blends at each end of the Y. The blends were mixes of human compounds. Compounds are mixes of different molecules. The scientists watched. What end of the Y did the mosquitoes go to?

After many tests, scientists found several compounds that mosquitoes did not like. The compounds repelled the mosquitoes. They drove them away. They repelled the mosquitoes as well as the sprays we buy. These compounds are present in only a small number of people.

How did the compounds repel the mosquitoes? Scientists think the compounds had a smell. It was strong. The strong smell masked the smell of other molecules. It covered it up. It masked the smell the mosquitoes liked. The mosquitoes were no longer attracted by smell. How will scientists use what they learned? Maybe they can make new sprays. The sprays will be based on human compounds. The sprays will repel mosquitoes.

Who Mosquitoes Like to Bite

After reading the story, answer the questions.
Fill in the circle next to the correct answer.

1. What are the smallest particles of matter?

   ⓐ atoms

   ⓑ space

   ⓒ compounds

   ⓓ molecules

2. This story is mainly about

   ⓐ molecules that smell.

   ⓑ scientists collecting data.

   ⓒ an experiment with mosquitoes.

   ⓓ atoms, molecules, and compounds.

3. Why was the tube shaped like a Y?

   ⓐ The scientists wanted to repel mosquitoes from both ends.

   ⓑ The scientists wanted to put more than one mosquito in each tube.

   ⓒ The scientists wanted to put the same blend in two different ends.

   ⓓ The scientists wanted the mosquito to make a choice between two smells.

4. Think about how the word **repel** relates to **attract**. Which words relate in the same way?

   repel : attract

   ⓐ mask : hide

   ⓑ hate : like

   ⓒ atom : small

   ⓓ scientist : data

5. What statement is true?

   ⓐ Mosquitoes are attracted to all people the same.

   ⓑ Scientists will use old sprays to repel mosquitoes.

   ⓒ Mosquitoes are not attracted to people if a certain smell is masked.

   ⓓ Scientists will use tubes in a Y shape in all experiments with mosquitoes.

How to Carry Water in a Net

New words to practice.

Say each word ten times.

❋ liquid	❋ evaporate
❋ definite	❋ evaporation
❋ volume	❋ condensation
❋ vapor	❋ particles

Choose one new word to write.

_____

- -

_____

How to Carry Water in a Net

You can't carry water in a net! Water is a liquid. A liquid is a state in which matter has a definite volume but no shape of its own. A liquid spreads out to fit the space it is in. A net has holes. If you put water in a net, it spills through the holes. It is impossible to carry water in a net!

Or is it? Matter is anything that takes up space and has weight. Matter can take three forms. Matter can be a liquid. Matter can be a solid. Matter can be a gas. A solid is a state that has a definite shape and volume. If you freeze water, it becomes a solid. Frozen water is still water. It is just in a different state. You can carry water in a net. You can carry water when it is a solid. You can carry water when it is frozen.

Water can also take the form of a gas. A gas is a state in which matter has no definite shape or volume. When water evaporates, it is turned into water vapor. It is turned into a gas in the air. Heat makes water evaporate. Heat can change water from a solid to a liquid to a gas.

Evaporation helps us to stay cool. When it gets hot, we sweat. Our sweat contains water in the liquid form. Our sweat evaporates into the air. This makes our skin feel cooler. Sometimes people use evaporation to get salt. They put salt water in special ponds. The sun heats up the water in the ponds. The water evaporates. It changes into water vapor. It changes into a gas. Salt is left behind!

The opposite of evaporation is condensation. Condensation is when a gas changes into a liquid. Fill a glass with ice and water. What happens? You will see tiny drops of water begin to form on the sides of the glass. Water vapor particles got close to the cold glass. The cold made particles in the gas slow down. The water vapor changed back into a liquid!

How to Carry
Water in a Net

After reading the story, answer the questions.
Fill in the circle next to the correct answer.

1. When water has a definite shape and volume, it is

   ⓐ in the form of sweat.

   ⓑ in the form of a gas.

   ⓒ in the form of a solid.

   ⓓ in the form of a liquid.

2. This story is mainly about

   ⓐ why we sweat.

   ⓑ water in three forms.

   ⓒ how liquids change to gas.

   ⓓ evaporation and condensation.

3. When warm air hits a cold window, would you expect droplets of water to form on the glass?

   ⓐ No, the water vapor in the air would condense on the glass.

   ⓑ Yes, the water vapor in the air would condense on the glass.

   ⓒ No, the water vapor in the air would evaporate on the glass.

   ⓓ Yes, the water vapor in the air would evaporate on the glass.

4. Think about how the word **evaporation** relates to **condensation**. What words relate in the same way?

evaporation : condensation

   ⓐ heat : gas

   ⓑ gas : vapor

   ⓒ bike : ride

   ⓓ gas : liquid

5. A puddle of water dries up. What happened to the water in the puddle?

   ⓐ It turned into a gas.

   ⓑ It turned into a solid.

   ⓒ It condensed into a gas.

   ⓓ It evaporated into a liquid.

Atoms and the Printing Press

New words to practice.

Say each word ten times.

* piece

* atom

* continue

* popular

* Greek

* copies

* unbreakable

* ancient

Choose one new word to write.

_____

- -

_____

Atoms and the Printing Press

Take a rock. Break it in half. Now take a piece and break it in half. Continue breaking each smaller piece of rock into smaller pieces. Could you continue forever? Is there some point where your rock is too small? Is there some point where it can no longer be broken?

Long ago, a Greek man thought about this. His name was Democritus. He was born in 460 B.C. Democritus's teacher thought there was a point where something could not get any smaller. Democritus wrote 72 books. He wrote how he agreed with his teacher. He wrote that the world was made up of very tiny pieces. The pieces were too small to be broken up. Democritus called these small pieces "atomos." In Greek, "atomos" means "unbreakable." In English, we say, "atom."

Long ago, books were copied by hand. It took a long time. Democritus's ideas were not popular. People did not like them. We do not have any copies of Democritus's books today. Why not? Only popular books were copied a large number of times. No one wasted time copying books no one wanted. How do we know about the books? Before the books were lost, another Greek read them. He was named Epicurus. Epicurus agreed with the books.

Epicurus wrote books, too. His books were copied less and less. Soon, they were all lost, just like Democritus's books. Before all Epicurus's books were lost, a Roman man read them. The Roman man agreed with the books. In about 56 B.C. he wrote a long poem. In the poem, he wrote about Democritus and Epicurus. He wrote about unbreakable atoms. In 1417, the only copy of this ancient poem was found.

We do not copy books by hand today. We use a printing press. A printing press was invented in 1454. A German man named Gutenberg invented it. When lots of copies of a book can be made, it is less likely for a book to disappear. The ancient poem about atoms was one of the first books to be put in printed form!

Atoms and the Printing Press

**After reading the story, answer the questions.
Fill in the circle next to the correct answer.**

1. This story is mainly about

   (a) rocks.

   (b) Democritus.

   (c) books about atoms.

   (d) the printing press.

2. In what year was the copy of the poem about atoms, Democritus, and Epicurus found?

   (a) 1417

   (b) 1454

   (c) 56 B.C.

   (d) 460 B.C.

3. Think about how the word **ancient** relates to **old**. Which words relate in the same way?

ancient : old

   (a) young : new

   (b) book : print

   (c) copies : hand

   (d) half : smaller

4. What answer lists events in the story in the right order or sequence?

   (a) Democritus writes a long poem; a Roman copies the poem.

   (b) Democritus agrees with his teacher; Epicurus writes books.

   (c) The printing press is invented; copies of Democritus's books are printed.

   (d) Democritus reads Epicurus' books; Epicurus's teacher agrees with Democritus.

5. If a lot of copies of a book are made, it is likely that

   (a) the book is not popular.

   (b) the book will not disappear.

   (c) the book was copied by hand.

   (d) the book is about unbreakable atoms.

Hot Monkeys

New words to practice.

Say each word ten times.

* geothermal   * mantle

* natural   * crust

* core   * geyser

* molten   * vegetables

Choose one new word to write.

_____

- -

_____

Hot Monkeys

Snow covers the ground. It is very cold. The monkeys in Japan are freezing! How are they going to survive the cold winter months? The monkeys know exactly what to do. They sit in steaming hot water. They sit in and by geothermal pools to keep warm.

Geothermal energy is a natural source of energy. It is a natural energy that escapes from inside the Earth. The word geothermal comes from two ancient Greek words. Geo means "of the Earth." Therme means heat. Geothermal energy is energy from our planet's heat.

It is hot inside our planet. The Earth is hottest at its inner core, or center. Scientists think the inner core is solid. It is made up of metal. The outer core is on top of the inner core. The outer core contains the same metals as the inner core. The metals are molten. Molten metals are in a melted state. The mantle is next. The mantle surrounds the outer core. The mantle is solid rock. The rock is very hot. The crust is on top of the mantle. We live on the crust. The crust is covered by soil, sand, and water.

Geothermal energy in the form of heat spreads from the center outward. Geothermal energy breaks through the crust in many ways. It can come out in the form of a volcano. It can come out in the form of a geyser. A geyser sends jets of hot water into the air. It can heat dirt. In some places in the Canary Islands, you can burn your fingers just by scraping away some of the soil! It heats pools of water, too.

Some countries have natural underground stores of hot water. Iceland uses its hot water to heat most of its homes and public buildings. The hot water runs through a system of pipes. The pipes direct the water under the streets. Iceland is a freezing cold country. Still, fresh vegetables and fruits grow there. The vegetables and fruits grow in greenhouses. The greenhouses are heated with geothermal energy.

Hot Monkeys

After reading the story, answer the questions.
Fill in the circle next to the correct answer.

1. How do monkeys in Japan survive the cold winter months?

   (a) They stay close to volcanoes.

   (b) They scrape away soil to find warm rocks.

   (c) They warm themselves in geothermal pools.

   (d) They get in jets of hot water called geysers.

2. What answer lists the Earth's layers in the correct order?

   (a) inner core, mantle, crust, outer core

   (b) mantle, crust, inner core, outer core

   (c) inner core, mantle, outer core, crust

   (d) inner core, outer core, mantle, crust

3. This story is mainly about

   (a) energy.

   (b) monkeys.

   (c) Iceland.

   (d) Earth's core.

4. In the story, you are told what the ancient Greek word geo means. Use what geo means to choose what a geologist would most likely study.

   (a) vegetables and fruits

   (b) land and water animals

   (c) rocks, fossils, and Earth's crust

   (d) light energy from stars and planets

5. Think about how the word **ice** relates to **water**. Which words relate in the same way?

ice : water

   (a) solid : core

   (b) core : solid

   (c) molten : rock

   (d) rock : molten

Floating Giants

New words to practice.
Say each word ten times.

* floating   * surface

* iceberg   * microscopic

* fields   * plankton

* calves   * capsizes

Choose one new word to write.

_____

- -

_____

Floating Giants

Something giant was floating in the water. It was bigger than Belgium, which is a country in Europe. It was over 200 miles (320 kilometers) long. It was over 60 miles (100 kilometers) wide. What was it?

The floating giant was an iceberg. It was first seen over 50 years ago. Icebergs are formed from fields of ice. The fields of ice cover the North Pole. They cover the South Pole, too. When a bit of ice breaks off, or calves, it becomes an iceberg. Icebergs are very heavy. Some weigh billions of pounds. How can these heavy giants float?

You see only a tiny part of an iceberg. Only about one-eighth floats above the surface of the water. The rest is below the surface of the water. Icebergs can float because they contain bubbles of oxygen. Oxygen is a gas. It is a gas in our air. The bubbles are microscopic. They are very small. Think about why a bottle can float. If a bottle is filled with air, it can float. The air bubbles keep the bottle afloat.

In an iceberg, the microscopic bubbles of oxygen have been trapped. They have been trapped for years and years. They have been trapped between layers of snow. The oxygen in the icebergs keeps them afloat in the water. The bubbles reflect light. They give icebergs their bright white color. Icebergs with less oxygen do not look as white. They look blue. They look like the blue of the polar sky.

Some icebergs have absorbed dirt and dust. The dirt and dust were carried in the air. The dirt and dust makes icebergs brown or black. Some icebergs are green! Plankton gives them the green color. Plankton are microscopic animals. Plankton floats in water. Animals and fish eat it. Green plankton freezes to the bottom of ice. When an iceberg calves, the green ice goes with it. As the iceberg melts, it capsizes. When it capsizes, it turns over. You see its lime green belly. Green icebergs are rare. Only one in a hundred icebergs are green.

Floating Giants

**After reading the story, answer the questions.
Fill in the circle next to the correct answer.**

1. This story is mainly about

   (a) the color of ice.

   (b) floating ice giants.

   (c) how heavy icebergs float.

   (d) an iceberg bigger than Belgium.

2. If your boat capsizes, you will

   (a) probably get wet

   (b) probably not know

   (c) probably trap plankton

   (d) probably see an iceberg

3. What causes some icebergs to be brown?

   (a) animals and fish eating it

   (b) plankton frozen to the ice

   (c) dust or dirt carried in the air

   (d) oxygen bubbles trapped in the snow

4. Why might a ship hit an iceberg?

   (a) Icebergs are rare.

   (b) Most of the iceberg cannot be seen.

   (c) Microscopic oxygen bubbles reflect light.

   (d) The iceberg may weigh billions of pounds.

5. Think about how the word **giant** relates to **big**. Which words relate in the same way?

giant : big

   (a) green : color

   (b) float : bubbles

   (c) iceberg : Belgium

   (d) microscopic : small

Ant Gliders

New words to practice.

Say each word ten times.

* swivels
* hind

* entomologist
* recorded

* arboreal
* flattened

* polish
* flanges

Choose one new word to write.

_____

- -

_____

Ant Gliders

High in a tree, an ant falls off. The ant does not fall any which way. Instead, the ant guides its fall. The ant quickly swivels. When something swivels, it turns. The ant turns itself completely around in midair. The ant swivels so it can glide backward to the tree.

How do we know this? Entomologists are scientists. They study insects. Some entomologists studied arboreal ants. If something is arboreal, it lives in trees. Entomologists studied arboreal ants in Panama, Costa Rica, and Peru. Panama and Costa Rica are in Central America. Peru is in South America.

The entomologists used nail polish. They used high-speed video cameras, too. The entomologists put nail polish on the ants' hind legs. Hind legs are back legs. The polish was white. It was white so it could be easily seen. Then, the entomologists dropped the ants. They dropped the ants from a height of 30 meters (about 100 feet). They recorded the ants' fall. They used the high-speed video cameras to record the fall.

Entomologists studied the ants' falls. They studied how ants control their body movements. Ants made the middle part of the bodies move in a special way. The middle part of their body seemed to move in waves. It had a wavy look. The ants used their hind legs. The hind legs were flattened. The ants used their flattened heads, too. The flattened heads had flanges. Flanges are flat parts that stick out. The flanges were used to steer. The ants used the flanges like rudders.

The entomologists recorded what the ants did after they landed, too. Did falling make the ants get lost? Most of the ants were not lost. They knew how to get home. They returned to their home tree. In fact, the ants returned to the same branch they had fallen from! How long did it take for the ants to get home? It took less than ten minutes! Entomologists think that ants sometimes fall on purpose. They fall to escape predators. They fall to escape danger.

Ant Gliders

After reading the story, answer the questions.
Fill in the circle next to the correct answer.

1. This story is mainly about
   - (a) falls.
   - (b) arboreal ants.
   - (c) entomologists.
   - (d) a way to escape predators.

2. What did the ants use to steer?
   - (a) flanges
   - (b) rudders
   - (c) hind legs
   - (d) the middle part of their body

3. Think about how the word **fall** relates to **escape**. Which words relate in the same way?

   | **fall : escape** |
   - (a) run: fun
   - (b) hind : back
   - (c) sleep : rest
   - (d) swivel : stay

4. What type of animal would most likely be arboreal?
   - (a) dog
   - (b) fish
   - (c) monkey
   - (d) elephant

5. What statement is true?
   - (a) All entomologists study insects.
   - (b) Some entomologists study insects.
   - (c) All scientists are entomologists.
   - (d) Some entomologists are scientists.

Dinosaur Data

New words to practice.

Say each word ten times.

✳ dinosaur	✳ weapons
✳ twice	✳ balance
✳ spikes	✳ giraffe
✳ armored	✳ serrated

Choose one new word to write.

_____

- -

_____

Dinosaur Data

Take a dinosaur that eats plants. Put it next to a same-sized dinosaur that eats meat. Which one would most likely have the longest legs? Think about your legs. If your legs were twice as long, you could take very big steps. You would be able to run very fast. Meat-eating dinosaurs needed to run fast. They needed to run fast to catch their prey. Meat-eating dinosaurs had the longest legs.

Take a dinosaur that has a tail with lumps of bone and spikes on it. Put it next to another dinosaur whose tail is smooth but twice as long. Which one most likely has the longest neck? Armored dinosaur tails were good weapons. The lumps of bone and spikes made good weapons. The dinosaur could use its armored tail to protect itself. Dinosaurs with long necks needed long tails to balance their weight. A dinosaur with a very long neck would need a very long tail to help balance its weight.

Take a giraffe, a mammal alive today. Take a plant-eating dinosaur long ago with a long neck. Why would both these animals have long necks? A giraffe's neck is about 8 feet (2.4 meters) long. Some dinosaurs had necks more than 30 feet (9 meters) long! The long necks on both animals served the same purpose. It made it easier to reach food. Both animals could eat high-up leaves.

Take a lizard, a reptile alive today. Take a dinosaur that could walk on two or four legs. Which animal has its legs under its body? All dinosaurs had legs under their bodies. This made their legs stronger. This made it so they could support more weight. It also made it easier to run.

Take a dinosaur with serrated teeth. Put it next to a dinosaur whose teeth are smooth. What one most likely eats meat? When something is serrated, it has notches in it. Saws have serrated edges. Steak knives have serrated edges, too. This makes it easier to cut something up. Meat-eating dinosaurs had serrated teeth to bite prey into pieces.

Dinosaur Data

**After reading the story, answer the questions.
Fill in the circle next to the correct answer.**

1. A dinosaur with long legs

   (a) has an armored tail.

   (b) has teeth with smooth edges.

   (c) can have its legs on the sides of its body.

   (d) can run faster than a dinosaur with short legs.

2. From the story you can tell that

   (a) no mammals are alive today.

   (b) some reptiles are alive today.

   (c) some dinosaurs are alive today.

   (d) no animals with serrated teeth are alive today.

3. This story is mainly about

   (a) armored dinosaurs.

   (b) meat-eating dinosaurs.

   (c) dinosaur body parts and what they do.

   (d) how dinosaurs are like reptiles alive today.

4. If you saw an animal without serrated teeth, it is likely that the animal

   (a) is a dinosaur.

   (b) has a long neck.

   (c) does not eat meat.

   (d) has its legs under its body.

5. Think about how the word **tail** relates to **balance**. Which words relate in the same way?

tail : balance

   (a) leg : fast

   (b) ear : hear

   (c) neck : long

   (d) serrated : smooth

Sharing Water with Predators

New words to practice.

Say each word ten times.

* tank	* dengue fever
* crustacean	* infected
* mosquito	* virus
* larvae	* predator

Choose one new word to write.

_____

- -

_____

Sharing Water with Predators

An lived in Vietnam. He lived in a small village. One of An's jobs was to go to the village water tank every day. An put water from the tank in his buckets. He carried the water home. One day, An's little sister Thu said that she wanted to go with An. "I am big," she said. "I want to help An carry water."

When they got to the tank, An held Thu up. He held her up so she could look into the tank. Thu let out a small cry. She jumped out of An's arms. She looked at An in horror. "An," she cried, "We cannot drink the water. There are animals in the water. I saw tiny animals swimming in the water. The water is not clean! We cannot drink dirty water."

An laughed. "Calm down, little sister," he said. He explained that the animals were put there on purpose. "They are crustaceans," he said. "Crustaceans are animals with a hard outer shell. Crustaceans usually live in the water. Shrimps and crabs are crustaceans. Lobsters are crustaceans, too. The crustaceans in our water are a special type. They were put there to eat mosquito larvae."

"No one in our village has gotten dengue fever in a long time," continued An. "Dengue fever is sometimes called 'breakbone fever.' This is because of how you feel when you are infected and sick. You feel great pain. Your joints get very stiff. Every year dengue fever causes over 50 million infections around the world. Every year at least 12,000 people die."

"Dengue fever is spread by mosquitoes. Mosquitoes spread the virus to us when they bite us. Mosquitoes lay eggs. The eggs hatch into larvae. The crustaceans in our water are predators. They eat the mosquito larvae! I know it is hard to drink water with predators swimming in it. But we need the predators to prey on the mosquito larvae. This is how we can control the mosquito population. This is how we can control the virus. This is how we can stop getting infected with dengue fever."

Sharing Water with Predators

After reading the story, answer the questions.
Fill in the circle next to the correct answer.

1. Dengue fever causes how many infections around the world every year?

   ⓐ over 12,000
   ⓑ over 50,000
   ⓒ over 12 million
   ⓓ over 50 million

2. This story is mainly about

   ⓐ mosquitoes.
   ⓑ a village in Vietnam.
   ⓒ one way to stop a virus.
   ⓓ animals called crustaceans.

3. What statement is true?

   ⓐ Crustaceans prey on mosquitoes.
   ⓑ Dengue fever cannot infect crustaceans.
   ⓒ Crustaceans kill the dengue fever virus.
   ⓓ Dengue fever is a virus spread by mosquitoes.

4. Think about how the word **village** relates to **city**. Which words relate in the same way?

   | **village : city** |

   ⓐ ant : one
   ⓑ pond : lake
   ⓒ eggs : water
   ⓓ mosquito : virus

5. Why did people in An's village put crustaceans in their water tanks?

   ⓐ They didn't mind drinking dirty water.
   ⓑ They needed to control the mosquito population.
   ⓒ They wanted mosquitoes to lay their eggs in the water.
   ⓓ They needed the crustaceans to prey on the dengue fever virus.

How a Telescope Led to Trouble

New words to practice.

Say each word ten times.

* arrested   * powerful

* sentence   * binoculars

* telescope   * galaxy

* observations   * universe

Choose one new word to write.

_____

- -

_____

How a Telescope Led to Trouble

Galileo was arrested. He was put in prison. He had to stay there for the rest of his life. When Galileo grew ill, his sentence was changed. It was changed to house arrest. Galileo could go home, but he could not go out. He had to stay home for the rest of his life. He could not ever leave. Why was Galileo arrested? Why was he given such a hard sentence?

Galileo was from Italy. He was born in 1564. He looked at the sky. He used a telescope. He made observations. His telescope was not very powerful. It was only as powerful as today's binoculars. Still, he could see many things. He could see more than he could with just his eyes. He saw mountains on our moon. He saw moons orbiting Jupiter.

People once thought the Sun orbited the Earth. A man said this was wrong. His name was Copernicus. He said Earth orbited the Sun. The Sun did not go around the Earth. This upset people in the Roman Catholic Church. They thought the Sun orbited the Earth. It was against the law to not agree with the Church. Galileo's observations made him agree with Copernicus. People in the Church were angry. They arrested Galileo. Today we know that Galileo was right. Earth orbits the Sun.

Telescopes today are very big. They are more powerful than today's binoculars! They allow us to see more. The more we can see, the more we can learn. We used to think there was only one galaxy. It was the Milky Way Galaxy. The Milky Way is our galaxy. Then, in 1923, a new telescope was built. Observations showed that the universe is made up of many galaxies.

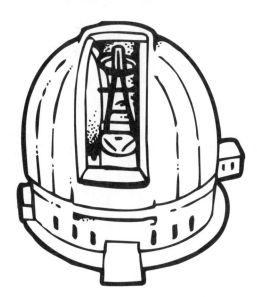

We learn by asking questions. We learn by making observations. Telescopes today are bigger than the one built in 1923. They are stronger. They can be put in space. They help us observe our universe. They help us learn more. Sometimes we learn new things. Sometimes we learn that what we thought was true is not true.

How a Telescope Led to Trouble

**After reading the story, answer the questions.
Fill in the circle next to the correct answer.**

1. What did Galileo's observations make him believe?

   ⓐ Copernicus was wrong.

   ⓑ Our moon orbited Jupiter.

   ⓒ The Sun orbited the Earth.

   ⓓ The Earth orbited the Sun.

2. This story is mainly about

   ⓐ Galileo and telescopes.

   ⓑ house arrest and Galileo.

   ⓓ galaxies and observations.

   ⓓ binoculars and telescopes.

3. When was Galileo born?

   ⓐ 1364

   ⓑ 1523

   ⓒ 1564

   ⓓ 1923

4. Think about how the word **observe** relates to **look**. Which words relate in the same way?

observe : look

   ⓐ kick : foot

   ⓑ ride : bike

   ⓒ sit : stand

   ⓓ sleep : rest

5. What statement would the author most likely agree with?

   ⓐ New observations are no longer needed.

   ⓑ Observations will not change what we know.

   ⓒ Some new observations may change what we know.

   ⓓ Observations should only be made with telescopes.

What You Burn

New words to practice.
Say each word ten times.

* calories   * batteries

* measure   * amounts

* stored   * digestive

* fuel   * delivers

Choose one new word to write.

_____

- -

_____

What You Burn

Walk for 20 minutes. You burn about 110 calories. Ride a bike for 20 minutes. You burn about 140 calories. Jump rope for 20 minutes. You burn about 210 calories. Jog for 20 minutes. You burn about 220 calories. What is a calorie? What are you burning?

A calorie is a measure of the energy value of food. It is a measure of how much energy a food can supply to your body. You use energy to breathe. You use it to move. You use it to digest your food. You use it even when you are sleeping. You need energy to keep going. You need lots of energy because you are growing. How much energy do you need? You need about 2,400 calories a day.

Stored energy can take many forms. Fuel is one form. Batteries are one form. Food is a form, too. Fuel and batteries are used to make machines go. You cannot use fuel or batteries to make you go. You cannot use energy stored in this form. You are not a machine. You are alive. You need energy stored in food.

Foods have different amounts of stored energy. A big egg has about 100 calories. A banana has about 100. So does one-half cup of cooked rice. A slice of bread has about 50 calories. A slice of chocolate cake has about 350. Drinks have different amounts, too. Whole milk has about 160 calories per cup. One cup of orange juice has about 110. Cans of soda pop may have 200 calories.

How do you get energy from food? First, you chew the food. You chew it into little bits. The bits go to the stomach. In the stomach, they are broken down. They are broken down into even smaller bits. Special digestive juices are used. This takes about five hours. Next, it goes to the small intestine. More digestive juices are added. The food bits get very tiny. They get small enough to pass into the blood. The blood travels all over your body. It delivers food. The blood delivers energy.

What You Burn

**After reading the story, answer the questions.
Fill in the circle next to the correct answer.**

1. About how many calories do you burn if you jump rope for 20 minutes?

   ⓐ 110

   ⓑ 140

   ⓒ 210

   ⓓ 220

2. This story is mainly about

   ⓐ food energy.

   ⓑ stored food.

   ⓒ burning food.

   ⓓ food digestion.

3. What happens after your food gets to your stomach?

   ⓐ It passes into the blood.

   ⓑ It is chewed into little bits.

   ⓒ It is broken down by digestive juices.

   ⓓ It is delivered all over your body after five hours.

4. Think about how the word **store** relates to **save**. Which words relate in the same way?

store : save

   ⓐ chew : digest

   ⓑ travel : stop

   ⓒ measure : burn

   ⓓ deliver : give

5. If you eat more calories than you burn up you will likely

   ⓐ get bigger.

   ⓑ get smaller.

   ⓒ stay the same.

   ⓓ stop storing energy.

Roy G. Biv and Light

New words to practice.

Say each word ten times.

✳ wavelengths	✳ laser
✳ indigo	✳ device
✳ absorbed	✳ seal
✳ memorize	✳ vessels

Choose one new word to write.

_____

- -

_____

Roy G. Biv and Light

Light is a form of energy. It moves in waves. Sunlight seems colorless. Light from an electric light bulb seems colorless, too. We call this white light. White light is really made up of many different colors. White light is made up of different wavelengths. White light is made up of the colors red, orange, yellow, green, blue, indigo, and violet. These colors all have different wavelengths.

The colors reflected by an object give it its color. Something that appears white reflects all colors of light. Something that appears yellow reflects only yellow light. The rest of the light colors are absorbed. Something that appears black does not reflect light at all. It absorbs all colors.

Red light has the longest wavelength. It has the longest distance between waves. Violet light has the shortest wavelength. It has the shortest distance between waves. It is easy to remember light colors by order of wavelength. Just memorize the name Roy G. Biv. The wavelength colors go in the same order as the letters in the name Roy G. Biv.

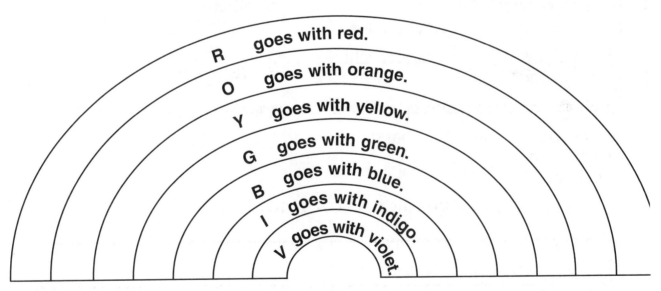

R goes with red.
O goes with orange.
Y goes with yellow.
G goes with green.
B goes with blue.
I goes with indigo.
V goes with violet.

Memorize, too, that the colors in Roy G. Biv go from those with the longest wavelength (red) to the shortest (violet).

A laser is a special device. It is a device that produces a beam of light. The light beam contains only one wavelength. The waves are all in step. They move along a single, narrow beam. Laser light is used for many things. Doctors sometimes use laser light. They use a needle-thin beam of light instead of a knife. The needle-thin beam of light produces heat. Heat from the laser light seals off any tiny blood vessels that have been cut. This means that a doctor can work fast. He does not have to stop to seal bleeding blood vessels.

Roy G. Biv and Light

After reading the story, answer the questions.
Fill in the circle next to the correct answer.

1. This story is mainly about

   (a) light.

   (b) lasers.

   (c) colors.

   (d) Roy G. Biv.

2. Why is the sky blue?

   (a) It only absorbs blue light.

   (b) It only reflects blue light.

   (c) It absorbs all light wavelengths.

   (d) It reflects only the shortest light wavelengths.

3. You can often see the light spectrum in a rainbow. What order of colors might you find in a rainbow?

   (a) yellow, green, red, violet

   (b) red, orange, violet, green

   (c) blue, orange, white, indigo

   (d) orange, yellow, green, blue

4. When something is sealed, it is

   (a) bleeding.

   (b) absorbed.

   (c) one wavelength.

   (d) closed tightly.

5. Think about how the word **reflect** relates to **absorb**. Which words relate in the same way?

reflect : absorb

   (a) sell : buy

   (b) boat : sink

   (c) laser : beam

   (d) light : energy

A Great Scientist

New words to practice.
Say each word ten times.

* inspector
* awarded
* obeying
* elements
* classmates
* radioactive
* research
* particles

Choose one new word to write.

_____

- -

_____

A Great Scientist

Marie Curie was born in Poland. She was born in 1867. At that time, Poland was under Russian rule. The Russian leaders said all school classes had to be taught in Russian. Children had to read Russian books. They had to learn Russian history. Marie went to a school where they read Polish books in secret. They learned Polish history.

One day there was a surprise visit. A Russian inspector came to check the school. The man was looking for teachers who were not teaching what the Russians wanted them to teach. He could send teachers away for not obeying. He could send students away for not obeying, too. He could send them all far, far away.

Marie and her classmates hid their Polish books. The inspector asked questions in Russian. Marie answered them. She answered in Russian. She answered correctly. The inspector did not know that Marie could have answered them in German, English, and French, too. Marie was only ten years old, but she helped save her teachers. She helped save her classmates.

Marie left Poland. She went to France. She worked hard. She wanted to be a scientist. She married another scientist. She became a doctor of science. She was the first woman in France to earn this degree. It took many years of school. It took many years doing research. Research is when you study something. You look into it. You find out new facts.

Nobel Prizes are awarded for great research. Marie was awarded two. She was the first person to earn two. Marie found two new elements. An element is a substance. It has only one type of atom. Marie's elements were radioactive. When something is radioactive, it gives off energy. The energy is in the form of particles or rays. The energy is the result of the atoms decaying or breaking up. Today we know these particles and rays are dangerous. Marie died in 1934. She died from cancer. The cancer was caused by her work with radioactive elements.

A Great Scientist

**After reading the story, answer the questions.
Fill in the circle next to the correct answer.**

1. This story is mainly about

   (a) research.

   (b) a scientist.

   (c) radioactive elements.

   (d) Poland under Russian rule.

2. Where did Marie become a doctor of science?

   (a) Poland

   (b) France

   (c) England

   (d) Germany

3. What was not true of the elements Marie found?

   (a) They gave off energy.

   (b) They were radioactive.

   (c) They only had one type of atom.

   (d) They took in particles and rays.

4. Why did the Russian inspector make a surprise visit?

   (a) He wanted to make sure the school was a good school.

   (b) He wanted to make sure Marie and her classmates were working hard.

   (c) He wanted to make sure the teachers were teaching what they were told to.

   (d) He wanted to make sure Marie could go to school for a long time and become a scientist.

5. Think about how the word **inspect** relates to **look**. Which words relate in the same way?

   | inspect : look |

   (a) award : prize

   (b) atom : element

   (c) particle : ray

   (d) research : study

The Hottest Eyes

New words to practice.
Say each word ten times.

* swordfish   * dissected

* organ   * temperature

* muscle   * movement

* circulated   * ocean

Choose one new word to write.

_____

- -

_____

The Hottest Eyes

Swordfish have a special heating organ. An organ is a part of an animal or plant that has a special purpose. Our heart is an organ. Our liver is an organ, too. The swordfish's heating organ is in a muscle. The muscle is near the eye.

Blood is circulated around the swordfish's eyes. When blood is circulated, it is moved around. The special heating organ heats the blood around the eyes. The circulating blood is like a heating blanket. It warms the eyes. Scientists have known that the blood was warmed. They did not know why.

They did an experiment to find out why. They went out on a boat. They caught ten swordfish. They dissected the swordfish eyes. When something is dissected it is cut apart. It is cut apart very carefully. The eyes were dissected right away. They were cut apart on the boat. The swordfish eyes were big. They were about the size of grapefruit.

The scientists did tests. The tests were on the eyes. The scientists flashed lights. They flashed lights at the eyes when they were different temperatures. The scientists found something. They found that the eyes could pick up fast movement more easily as they warmed up. How high could swordfish warm their eyes? Up to 27 degrees Fahrenheit (about 13 degrees Celsius) above the temperature of the ocean! How well could the warmed eyes see? They could see movement 10 times faster.

Tuna have the same heating organ. Sharks have it, too. The swordfish's heating organ is bigger than the tuna's. It is bigger than the shark's, too. What animal hunts in the coldest water? Is it the tuna? Is it the shark? Or is it the swordfish? Think about what fish has the biggest heating organ. The swordfish can warm its eyes the most. Its eyes can see movement fast in cold water. This makes it so the swordfish can hunt in more parts of the ocean.

The Hottest Eyes

**After reading the story, answer the questions.
Fill in the circle next to the correct answer.**

1. This story is mainly about

   ⓐ how to see movement in cold water.

   ⓑ how blood circulates around the eye.

   ⓒ how and why swordfish warm their eyes.

   ⓓ how tuna, sharks, and swordfish are the same.

2. If a scientist carefully cuts open a plant to look at its insides, you could say that the scientist has

   ⓐ warmed the plant.

   ⓑ dissected the plant.

   ⓒ circulated the plant.

   ⓓ done an experiment on the plant.

3. Think about how the word **warmest** relates to **coldest**. What words relate in the same way?

   | warmest : coldest |

   ⓐ different : same

   ⓑ eye : grapefruit

   ⓒ flash : experiment

   ⓓ circulate : around

4. Why can the swordfish hunt in more parts of the ocean than tuna or sharks?

   ⓐ It has a special heating organ.

   ⓑ It has eyes the size of grapefruit.

   ⓒ It can circulate warmed blood around its eyes.

   ⓓ It can warm its eyes more than tuna or sharks.

5. What might be one reason why the scientists did the experiment on the boat?

   ⓐ They were far out in the ocean.

   ⓑ They needed to test the eyes in the coldest water.

   ⓒ They wanted to catch as many swordfish as they could.

   ⓓ They needed to look at the eyes before they got too old.

Answer Sheets

Student Name: _____

Title of Reading Passage: _____

1. (a)   (b)   (c)   (d)

2. (a)   (b)   (c)   (d)

3. (a)   (b)   (c)   (d)

4. (a)   (b)   (c)   (d)

5. (a)   (b)   (c)   (d)

Student Name: _____

Title of Reading Passage: _____

1. (a)   (b)   (c)   (d)

2. (a)   (b)   (c)   (d)

3. (a)   (b)   (c)   (d)

4. (a)   (b)   (c)   (d)

5. (a)   (b)   (c)   (d)

Bibliography

Asimov, Isaac. *How Did We Find Out About Atoms?* Walker and Company, 1976.

Berman, Bob. "Earth's Other Sister." *Discover.* April, 2004: 30.

Biel, Timothy Levi. *Zoobooks: Turtles.* Wildlife Education, Ltd., 1993.

Brust, Beth Wagner, and Dorn, Bob. *Zoobooks: Rattlesnakes.* Wildlife Education, Ltd., 1989.

Casselman, Anne. "For the Eyes Only." *Discover.* May, 2005: 17.

Cho, Shinta. *The Gas We Pass: The Story of Farts.* Kane/Miller Book Publishers, 1994.

Choi, Charles Q. "Crustaceans Against Dengue Fever." *Scientific American.* April, 2005: 34.

———. "Descent of the Ants." *Scientific American.* April, 2005: 34.

Cole, Ron. Stephen Hawking: *Solving the Mysteries of the Universe.* Steck-Vaughn Company, 1997.

Cromwell, Sharon. *Why Does My Tummy Rumble When I'm Hungry? and Other Questions About the Digestive System.* Reed Educational & Professional Publishing, 1998.

Darling, David. *Making Light Work: the Science of Optics.* Dillon Press, Macmillan Publishing Company, 1991.

"dengue," *The New Encyclopedia Britannica*, volume 4, page 12. Encyclopedia Britannica, Inc, 1990.

Fisher, Leonard Everett. *Marie Curie.* Macmillan Publishing Company, 1994.

Fullick, Ann. *Marie Curie.* Heinemann Library, Reed Educational & Professional Publishing, 2001.

Gedatus, Gus. *Exercise for Weight Management.* Capstone Press, 2001.

Graham, Ian. *Solar Power.* Raintree Steck-Vaughn Publishers, 1999.

———. Wind Power. Raintree Steck-Vaughn Publishers, 1999.

Hidalgo, Maria. *Light.* Creative Education, 2003.

Jacobs, William. "Digital Sundials." *Discover.* April, 2004: 78.

Jaffe, Mark. *And No Birds Sing: A True Ecological Thriller Set in a Tropical Paradise.* Barricade Books, Inc., 1997.

Jedrosz, Aleksander. *Eyes.* Troll Associates, 1992.

Kahn, Jennifer. "Monsters on Ice." *Discover.* March, 2004: 52-59.

Kallen, Stuart. A. *Icebergs.* Kidhaven Press, Thomson Learning, Inc., 2003.

Kerrod, Robin. *New Materials.* Smart Apple Media, 2004.

Kinch, Michael P. *Warts.* Franklin Watts, Grolier Publishing Company, 2000.

Bibliography

Leokum, Arkady. *Tell Me Why #2.* Grosset & Dunlap, 1986.

Miles, Lisa, and Smith, Alastair. *The Usborne Complete Book of Astronomy & Space.* Scholastic, Inc., 1998.

Morgan, Ben. *Gases.* Blackbirch Press, 2003.

Mowat, Farley. *Never Cry Wolf.* Bantam Books, 1979.

Netting, Jessa Forte. "Hidden in Plain Sight." *Discover.*

April, 2005: 10.

Overbeck, Cynthia. *Carnivorous Plants.* Lerner Publications Company, 1982.

Preston, Richard. "Climbing the Redwoods." *The New Yorker.* February 14 & 21, 2005: 212-225.

Rickard, Graham. *Geothermal Energy.* Gareth Stevens, Inc., 1991.

Selim, Jocelyn. "Mosquito Barricade." *Discover.* April, 2005: 11.

Silverstein, Alvin and Virginia, and Nunn, Silverstein Laura. *Symbiosis.* Twenty-First Century Books, 1998.

Spilsbury, Louise. *Why Should I Eat this Carrot? And Other Questions About Healthy Eating.* Heinemann Library, Reed Elsevier, Inc., 2003.

Steele, Christy. *Tsunamis.* Steck-Vaughn Company, 2002.

Topp, Michael R. "How are the Abbreviations of the Periodic Table Determined?" *Scientific American.* February, 2005: 106.

Tsubakiyama, Margaret. *Lice are Lousy! All About Headlice.* The Millbrook Press, Inc., 1999.

Vogt, Gregory. *Stars and Constellations.* Steck-Vaughn Company, 2001.

Wexo, John Bonnett. *Prehistoric Zoobooks: Book Seven.* Wildlife Education, Ltd., 1989.

——-. *Zoobooks: Eagles.* Wildlife Education, Ltd., 1993.

——-. *Zoobooks: Night Animals.* Wildlife Education, Ltd., 1991.

——-. *Zoobooks: Seals and Sea Lions.* Wildlife Education, Ltd., 1992.

Answer Key

Page 11—Snake Sense
1.a 2.d 3.d 4.c 5.b

Page 14—At the Top of Giants
1.c 2.a 3.b 4.b 5.a

Page 17—Moon Tricks
1.a 2.d 3.b 4.d 5.a

Page 20—Not Nice Lice
1.c 2.c 3.d 4.b 5.b

Page 23—Seeing Colors at Night
1.b 2.d 3.c 4.d 5.a

Page 26—Adding Up an Elephant
1.b 2.a 3.d 4.d 5.a

Page 29—A 200,000 Year-Old Meal
1.b 2.d 3.c 4.d 5.b

Page 32—A Riddle
1.c 2.a 3.a 4.b 5.d

Page 35—All About Air
1.a 2.d 3.d 4.b 5.c

Page 38—Burning Ships
1.c 2.c 3.d 4.a 5.a

Page 41—A True Life Mystery
1.c 2.b 3.a 4.b 5.c

Page 44—Hunter in the Sky
1.d 2.b 3.c 4.b 5.a

Page 47—Strange Partners
1.a 2.c 3.a 4.d 5.b

Page 50—Warts
1.a 2.b 3.d 4.a 5.b

Page 53—The Fastest Thing in the Universe
1.b 2.d 3.a 4.a 5.b

Page 56—Turtle or Tortoise?
1.b 2.d 3.c 4.d 5.c

Page 59—Hidden Treasure—Right Before Our Eyes!
1.a 2.b 3.c 4.d 5.d

Page 62—Where You Can Run Away From Night
1.b 2.a 3.a 4.c 5.c

Page 65—Meat-Eating Plants
1.b 2.a 3.c 4.c 5.b

Page 68—Harnessing the Wind
1.d 2.d 3.a 4.c 5.a

Page 71—A Dinner of Mice
1.c 2.a 3.b 4.d 5.c

Page 74—How to See Through a Wall
1.c 2.a 3.a 4.b 5.d

Page 77—Night Animals
1.a 2.c 3.c 4.d 5.b

Page 80—What the Letters Mean
1.d 2.c 3.c 4.d 5.b

Page 83—The Midnight Sun
1.b 2.c 3.d 4.a 5.b

Page 86—Passing Gas
1.b 2.a 3.d 4.a 5.c

Page 89—The Walrus
1.b 2.b 3.a 4.c 5.d

Page 92—Clothes Stronger than Steel
1.c 2.b 3.a 4.c 5.d

Page 95—Tsunami
1.d 2.b 3.d 4.b 5.a

Page 98—Flying Predators
1.d 2.a 3.b 4.c 5.c

Page 101—The Gas Giant
1.a 2.d 3.a 4.b 5.c

Page 104—Who Mosquitoes Like to Bite
1.a 2.c 3.d 4.b 5.c

Page 107—How to Carry Water in a Net
1.c 2.b 3.b 4.d 5.a

Page 110—Atoms and the Printing Press
1.c 2.a 3.a 4.b 5.b

Page 113—Hot Monkeys
1.c 2.d 3.a 4.c 5.d

Page 116—Floating Giants
1.b 2.a 3.c 4.b 5.d

Page 119—Ant Gliders
1.b 2.a 3.c 4.c 5.a

Page 122—Dinosaur Quiz
1.d 2.b 3.c 4.c 5.b

Page 125—Sharing Water with Predators
1.d 2.c 3.d 4.b 5.b

Page 128—How a Telescope Led to Trouble
1.d 2.a 3.c 4.d 5.c

Page 131—What You Burn
1.c 2.a 3.c 4.d 5.a

Page 134—Roy G. Biv and Light
1.a 2.b 3.d 4.d 5.a

Page 137—A Great Scientist
1.b 2.b 3.d 4.c 5.d

Page 140—The Hottest Eyes
1.c 2.b 3.a 4.d 5.d